DIAMOND
CUTTERS

DIAMOND CUTTERS

VISIONARY
POETS
IN
AMERICA
BRITAIN
& OCEANIA

EDITED
& INTRODUCED BY

ANDREW HARVEY
& JAY RAMSAY

SMOOTH STONES PRESS

COPYRIGHT

Edited by Nora Boxer
Cover Photographs courtesy Shutterstock
Cover Design Wabi Sabi Design Group (WSDG)

THE POETS

Lewis Thompson

David Gascoyne

Kathleen Raine

William Stafford

Sally Purcell

Robert Bly

Andrew Harvey

Dorothy Walters

Jeni Couzyn

Janine Canan

Charles Upton

Alan Jackson

Jehanne Mehta

Jennifer Doane Upton

Gabriel Bradford Millar

Paul Matthews

Sebastian Barker

Aidan Andrew Dun

Thanissara

Hilary Davies

Niall McDevitt

Rose Flint

Jay Ramsay

Zanna Beswick

Peter Owen Jones

Alan Rycroft

Henry Shukman

Georgi Y. Johnson

Ivan M. Granger

Mirabai Starr

Irina Kuzminsky

Jenny D'Angelo

Diana Durham

Chris Saade

Philip Wells

Lisa Page

Helen Moore

Thomas R. Smith

John Fox

Anna Saunders

Victoria Field

Kim French

ANDREW'S DEDICATION:

For all who care to know.

The day when we get back to the ancient worship of delight
and beauty will be our day of salvation; for without these
things there can be neither an assured nobility and sweetness
in poetry and art, nor a satisfied dignity and fullness of life,
nor a harmonious perfection of the spirit.

— **Sri Aurobindo, "The Future of Poetry"**

JAY'S DEDICATION:

For Gillian Kean, founder of Hazelwood & fearless sacred activist (d. 2013)

And in memory of John Gibbens, brother poet & folk troubadour (d. 2015)

Remember, remember the love
Like a great rainbow balancing
Colours within and without
Encompassing all points
Above below and throughout.

Remember, remember the tunnel
However dark it might seem
Has light at the end of it,
And we are the light and the tunnel.

Remember, remember the bright
And glowing ember,
That life rubs mind and heart together
And the fire of joy can leap between
And clothe us in our own true garment.

— G.K. (1996)

TABLE CONTENTS

DIAMOND CUTTERS

INTRODUCTION BY ANDREW HARVEY

This anthology, that I have co-edited with my friend Jay Ramsay, is the realization of a long, passionately held, dream—to offer to all those who want it an electric overview of the pioneering visionary poetry in English over the last hundred years.

As our world sinks deeper and deeper into moral and spiritual nihilism, lethal fundamentalism, economic, social, and environmental chaos and collapse, a small, scattered, largely obscure cohort of brave, wild, vulnerable, impassioned spirits has kept alive the flame of divine inspiration and so ensured that the most ancient role of the poet—to be a servant of divine truth and beauty and revealer of reality—has survived and even thrived, despite derision from official tastemakers who have outlawed the sublime, and despite a contemporary poetry world, addicted to cheap irony, unearned despair, bizarre pastiche, narcissistic confessionalism, and blindingly boring baroque word games. *Diamond Cutters* celebrates the illumined heroism of this band of lonely adventurers of the sacred heart and offers their testimony to the subtle splendors of spiritual knowledge and ecstasy to all those famished for truth in a world of lies.

Nothing is more important—or more difficult to obtain—in our abject time than authentic inspiration. Without such an inspiration drawn from the highest realms of sacred truth, those known and mapped in the world's great mystical traditions and aflame in the work of seer-poets like Vyasa, Dante, Rumi, Kabir,

Basho, Whitman, Blake, and Rilke, humanity will lose heart in the exploding horror it has created out of its own hubris and destroy itself and a large part of nature. The poets that Jay and I have gathered together in *Diamond Cutters* know this searing truth; it is this knowledge that has driven them in their often unrewarded missions to keep trying to reach an increasingly deaf humanity with the still potentially all transforming good news of its innate divinity. The poets Jay and I have chosen are each aware that humanity stands at a threshold where, as Teilhard de Chardin wrote, "We will have to choose between adoration and suicide." They have, at whatever cost to their personal lives or literary careers, chosen the witness of adoration —adoration of the divine itself, often beyond dogma or formal religion, adoration of the divine magnificence of nature, adoration of the humble holy splendor of human life lived consciously as a divine gift and responsibility.

Such witness is especially precious in a time like ours when formal religion has lost its appeal for millions of people who still remain hungry for, and open to, transforming spiritual truth. For those with the eyes to see, the poets of *Diamond Cutters* have each in their own unique way shouldered the strange role our evolutionary crisis offers them—that of making vivid, vibrant, personal and accessible the essential eternal truths of divine transcendence and eminence, of a cosmos secretly brilliant with presence and of a humanity created in the image of the divine and graced with the original blessing of divine consciousness. Increasingly illumined themselves, they have learned how to pour out for us the treasures divine love has poured into them with passion, joy, wit, linguistic lucidity and brilliance, and the kind of vulnerable honesty that helps us to believe and trust what they say.

Such brave sacred work demands a brave and sacred approach from those who read it. Sri Aurobindo in "The Future Poetry" defines the sacred poet as "a soul expressing the eternal spirit of Truth and Beauty through some of the infinite variations of Beauty with the word for its instrument." He adds, "It is to a similar soul in us seeking the same spirit and responding to it that he makes his appeal." Sacred poetry is not entertainment and cannot be approached or understood from the unillumined intellect; it can only yield its secrets to and awaken its mysteries in those prepared to bring to its encounter the awed, humble intention of their spirit and its longing for union with reality, the deepest possible commitment of their whole being to the rigors and revelations of authentic transformation.

Let us then, dear friends, find our own faces in the mirror of the courage that this anthology represents; let us continue to do the unsparing inner work necessary to understand and integrate the truths and challenges that flash from their words; let us honor these poets' epiphanies and claim and remember our own with growing gratitude; let us, whatever happens, hold to their nobility of celebration and praise so that all we are and all we do, in whatever circumstances we may find ourselves, can be invigorated, refined, and perpetually refreshed by the ecstasy, energy, clarity and dynamic peace that stream forever towards us from the unborn and undying Light

Andrew Harvey
May 2016, Chicago

INTRODUCTION BY JAY RAMSAY

Why is poetry important, even essential, for us now ? And what part does it have to play in the wider culture of our time?

Answering this question is what has given rise to this anthology between Andrew and myself at this time, decided as we walked slowly up and down the long drive up to Hawkwood College in Gloucestershire, late one early September evening; the fields and valley below, the spread of the stars above.

Poetry has always held both the stories and the consciousness of the tribe, reaching deep into what we know as the Oral Tradition—and as Julian Jaynes suggests in his extraordinary book *The Origins of Consciousness in the Breakdown of the Bicameral Mind* (1976) about language and prophecy, for longer than prose. Poetry and music both speak to the same part of the brain, which actually (as recent neuroscientific research has indicated) is a *different* part of the brain than prose speaks to. It is the lyrical, of course, and also the imaginal. It is the imagination, which gives rises to vision, which is central and at stake here. As the saying goes

'Without a vision, the people perish'

David Gascoyne, the second poet (1.) featured in this anthology, an exceptional poet rated by one contributor here as 'the real T.S. Eliot', (2.) spoke of poets as being the 'antennae of their culture and time'. *In his Prelude to a New Fin de Siecle,* conceived back in the 1980's as one of the last things he wrote, he also describes the poet as a 'seismograph': an exceptionally sensitive and accurate recording instrument. So what of a culture that doesn't listen seriously to its poets—especially its poets who are worth listening to because they address the real questions of our time within the bigger picture of our time ? What happens to that culture and its people ?

Our time as we know, and as Andrew Harvey perhaps knows and speaks of publicly better than anyone, is a time of transition and crisis: crisis and opportunity. Awakening and consciousness, not just of the individual but of whole groups and communities, in short, the collective, is imperative as we know. The evidence is all around. We have had great individuals: a great individual, Nelson Mandela, was recently laid to rest. Now we need great *movements*—we need inspired, awakened people. This is what some governments fear the most, of course. (The evidence for that is also more available than ever).

People are confused about poetry, largely as a result of Modernism in the early 20th C. and its double-edged sword. Modernism extended the reach of poetry, and it 'modernized' it; no question: but it also brought poetry more and more into the hands of the few away from the hands of the many. Nobody seriously complained about poetry being inaccessible at the time of Byron or Shelley. The complaints were about their politics perhaps, as well as their private lives, but certainly not about the accessibility of their writing. Modernism changed all that; and Eliot's 'The Waste Land' (1922), for all its splendour and visionary integrity, was also part of that, and the increasing academicization that grew up around it, the endless studies, the footnotes to footnotes. Eliot himself moved forward: *Four Quartets* is a deeply accessible poem, much more widely read. The greatest poets—Tagore, Yeats, Gibran— have never simply written for a chosen few, or even just for other poets out of some kind of ever-modernizing excuse: it would be unthinkable to them, or to any poet serious about having and addressing an audience for the sake of raising consciousness and awareness.

The academicization of poetry, fed by university programmes as well as poets themselves within these programmes who are narcissistically desperate to be seen as 'original' and 'new' has in many ways reduced poetry to a minor sport. How many people read, for example, Language Poetry simply for pleasure or enlightenment ? Again and again I have heard audiences talk to me of their love of poetry and their disappointment at a lot of what it has become. It just doesn't speak to them. And they want it to.

But more than that, its lack of spiritual content and vision, even its determined autonomy and anti-mystical atheism has created a particular linguistic materialism where language *in the absence of God* is held to be sufficient unto itself. Result ? Obscurity, as well as a lack of transparency—the transparency necessary that lets in something more than just words, rather as a stained glass window lets in light. I am not saying that poetry can never or should never be 'difficult'—the deep and dark things of life are clearly difficult and challenging and we need poetry than can address those things just as we need psychotherapy and healing that can address those things. But the obscurity of poetic syntax *for its own sake* is not simply difficult—

it is actually unreadable, because it serves only itself. Like smoke gathering under a ceiling, it has nowhere to go. The house it dwells in has no skylights !

As Janine Canan, another of our contributors, reflects in a short poem called 'Imposters' from her collection *Ardor* included here (3.):

> What makes these so-called poems ?
> Not poets ! Machines toying
> With parts, vampires sucking blood
>
> From words instead of shedding it,
> Strangling language since they have
> Nothing to say or praise.

She's devastatingly accurate. If poetry 'always has something unsayable to say' as Michele Roberts, poet, novelist and feminist once memorably suggested to me, then surely this lack of content and praise is it !

But not the 40 or so poets gathered here, and certainly not the poetry and the tradition they represent—a distinct thread that originates in British as well as German Romanticism with Blake, Wordsworth, Keats, Shelley; and which also shines in Whitman, Jeffers, and Ginsberg closer to our time. Romanticism is the radical movement *par excellence* in poetry in the face of mind-identified Reason it revolts against in service of the heart and Nature. It is the seeding ground of all radical, cutting-edge and relevant poetry today which is why its originators remain legendary; and why in England today we hold Blake as our timeless Laureate, as well as celebrating his birthday (November

28th). The other thread that is vital in this visionary emphasis here owes its origin to French Symbolism and the work of Baudelaire and Arthur Rimbaud in France in the 1870's, an emphasis that has touched all the poets writing here because of their witnessing to what is possible through the imagination as an extension of our ordinary perceptions, and as a result, our ways of thinking. Rimbaud in particular, like Blake, remains an inspirational source with his particular blazing honesty. As he says in his famous letter of May 1871 (to Paul Demeny) (4.):

I say you have to be a visionary, make yourself a visionary.

He details an internal alchemy of external recognition and internal distillation in which he affirms that we will need 'the greatest faith'; in his language, the poet is a supreme outsider: 'For he attains the unknown !'. For Rimbaud, this is soul work, that both takes him to the edge and to prophecy. As he goes on to say, very relevantly for our time:

And there will be poets like this ! When the eternal slavery of Women is destroyed, when she lives for herself and through herself, when man—up till now abominable —will have set her free, she will be a poet as well ! Woman will discover the unknown ! Will her world of ideas differ from ours ? She will discover strange things, unfathomable, repulsive, delightful; we will accept and understand them.

That prediction has certainly come, and remains, true.

Paradoxically, poetry has also had a resurgence of popularity in the last thirty years, no question: as a result of poets who have had the humility as well as the passion to be popular, to write for people rather than 'against' them as lesser and less-educated beings. As Adrian Mitchell, the most political of them here in England, put it succinctly:

Most people ignore most poetry
because most poetry ignores most people. (5.)

This emphasis, with its spoken word aspect rooted in the radicalism of the 1960's and then the '80's (when my own work with the Angels of Fire festivals in London began), is also reflected stylistically in what is gathered here, where we can see that poetry, because it is 'speakable,' is also understandable. It is communication rather than solipsism. And our capacity to communicate now as poets writing now is vital if we are to contribute to the great transition of our time. What is also happening politically as well as socially takes on a new significance when we can see it symbolically as well as literally in world events as they are unfolding, something I've tried to witness in my own recent writing. This learning to 'read the world' is what poetry is uniquely equipped to do. All of the poets represented here recognize that abundantly, which is also why they are able to meaningfully explore the parallel art forms of music and film which hold so much potential for where poetry is continuing to develop new horizons.

But I want to quote someone else, someone rather less well known and unexpected who has something very penetrative to say about all this in a spiritual context: a Mongolian shaman-poet called Galsan Tschinag (6.). *In his Defence of Poetry 1999; Defence of the Stone against Plaster*, this is what he has to say:

> Poetry is an enormous counterforce against the oppressing weight of the material world. It is a spice in every day life, a sting against habit; it changes life, which is more and more outweighed by consumption. Poetry, after all, belongs to the side of the heart in opposition to the stomach...

He has something even stronger to say about poets themselves as well as their potential audience, which also makes the point about why poetry is so important for us now:

> With those people who have an overfed stomach, poetry has a hard time. Like our inner parts, so are our thoughts. From disturbed, dulled thoughts springs disturbed, weakened poetry. The reduction of poetry to decoration, as part of consumption, chopped-up prose, the unimaginative, pathetic play with form, the shameless, shallow pomposity about truism, the stringing together of sentences that are grammatically correct but dead in their structure—a pseudo-poetry, produced on a massive scale almost like shoes, hamburgers and non-returnable bottles, but with one decisive consequence: it annoys the reader and kills their feeling for poetry...

People haven't lost their love of poetry, but they have lost their faith that it can deliver. *Diamond Cutters* is all for those people, and it's why it has the title it does. This is what Andrew and I wanted to achieve: a gathering of spiritually, aesthetically and ecologically conscious contemporaries who together prove that poetry is not only relevant, it is absolutely readable and deeply exciting as well as satisfying and uplifting. It is also capable, like any shaman (or woman), of plunging to the divinized depths.

As Ivan M. Granger, founder of the Poetry Chaikhana website in Colorado with its focus on Sacred Poetry from around the world, phrases it in his recent anthology *The Longing In Between* (7.):

> Poetry has an immediate effect on the mind. The simple act of reading poetry alters thought patterns and the shuttle of the breath. Poetry induces trance. Its words are chant. Its rhythms are drumbeats. Its images become the icons of the inner eye. Poetry is more than a description of the sacred experience; it carries the experience itself.

As a result of my work as a psychotherapist for over more than 20 years, which followed and accompanied my primary vocation as a poet, I've come to see how the authentic self and 'the poet inside us' are part of the same thing: that *primary voice* that really holds the soul and truthful expression of all we are and can be. My own work, which includes my correspondence course book *The Poet in You* (8.), is an expression of this emphasis, also in many workshops as well as events and performances, in which I've seen the healing as well as enlivening power of poetry at first hand. This is where—to extend Tschinag's metaphor—*the stone is freed of its plaster* to stand and breathe. Poetry stands against the compromise of our authentic selves in the public sector, and so it joins our refusal to be inauthentic which is the mass movement of our time, refined in the form that Andrew has also named and celebrated as 'sacred activism'. The real poetry of our time is just that, written and lived, and so are its authors.

We are 'pilgrims of truth' if we have any truthfulness and direction in our lives, obedient and intuitively responsive to something greater than ourselves which reaches into the vastness as well as mystery of the spiritual world. Poetry, as Shelley always recognized, is our spiritual path here.

All my previous five anthologies of Contemporary Poetry since 1986—*Angels of Fire, Transformation, Earth Ascending, Into the Further Reaches*, and *Soul of the Earth*—bear witness to this. *Diamond Cutters*, the sixth, holds the most synthesis between its elements as well as its contributors, whose birthdays span a century beside this present moment of time. And these poets, who are among the finest writing on both sides of the Atlantic (some of whom, like David Whyte, have also relocated from one side to the other) are harbingers too; of a new wave—also of new and as yet unknown younger generation names—which is breaking into our conscious awareness with all its promise of transformation as well as healing of the human being reunited in heart as well as mind...celebrating the body as the vessel as well as gift of life itself *within all that in reality is Divine*. This is the time.

Many of these poets, as you can see from their biographies at the back of the book, are also working with healing and therapeutic work of one kind or another, as well as poetry; within a new paradigm I named around the millennium as 'the artist-healer'. This actually changes the identity of 'the poet', as well as poetry as we've known it and at the beginning (still) of a new century which the last century has held as vision and potential, even in its darkest hours where humanity's shadow still holds so much weight.

May you find its secret song, its light and fire, in these pages. May they flame within you. As another of them, the Cambridge poet Richard Berengarten (9.) relevantly suggests:

Fulcrum of diamond, balancing between
each thing and thing, space each thing must evince,
we cannot track you, but infer you, since
you are the means by which all things are seen,
pouring *now*, overbrimming, into *this*
measuring *this, this,* on your weightlessness.

Jay Ramsay
May 2016
Stroud, Gloucestershire, UK

References

1. *Prelude to a New Fin de Siecle (Greville Press, 1984)*
2. *remark by Niall McDevitt in Porterloo (International Times, 2013)*
3. *Ardor by Janine Canan (Pilgrims Publishing, Varanasi, 2012)*
4. *Arthur Rimbaud, Complete Works, trans. Paul Schmidt (Harper Colophon, USA, 1976) p.102-3*
5. *Adrian Mitchell in For Beauty Douglas (Allison & Busby, 1982)*
6. *Galsan Tschinag in Into the Further Reaches, ed. JR (PS Avalon, Glastonbury, 2007)*
7. *www.poetry-chaikhana.com*
8. *Jay Ramsay, The Poet in You (O Books, 2009)*
9. *from 'To light, an interior': sonnet by Richard Berengarten*

DIAMOND CUTTERS

THE DOUBLE LIPS

The double lips betray
One tongue to endless words.
One not repeated never was:
Avoid the same new lie.

No one new moment nude
Survives the Lightning-flash —
Heaven shut on the flight of a bird,
Bone born before the flesh.

The fourfoot Unicorn
Uproots all biped thought;
The Three-eyed God makes light
Of mirrored sun and moon.

. . . Folly repairs what wisdom sifted raw:
New grass grows over the rusted oven.
And Samson conquered with an ass's jaw:
Logic weighs air: the scales end always even.

THE MANGO-TREES

Under the rich, self-dreaming mango-spires
Scented like satyr loves and milky seas,
The frozen spiky foam of moonlight fires,
Falls to the core of earth an indigo night of leaves.

The naked heart of love, rich, simple, rare,
Unmeasured sweetness, grave, most delicate,
In golden plumes dusk with redoubled light
Given over beyond recall upon the common air.

An amber cloud deepens to secrecy
So open a dream its heaven eludes the sense
And all that rapture, all that ecstasy
Becomes its own pure angel, mute with radiance.

LEWIS THOMPSON

UNDERWORLD

Demons disturb my day.
        The underworld floods up:
Its dark prehistory
        Would drain me like a cup.

Dark earth-womb, you abhor
        The kindling quick of light
And every lucid flower
        Doom back to cold night.

The waveless flood, Lethe,
        The desperate living head
Breathing, drowns memory –
        Baptism of the dead.

The hungry, unavenged.
        Every cold-shouldered ghost
Our heartless laugh estranged
        Betrays us: we are lost.

The shrieking mandrake-root
        Rung from a voiceless bell! –
How shall our flower and fruit
        Master descent to hell?

LEWIS THOMPSON

THE HEART OF THE WORLD

All that can melt has melted: only jewels,
That in the heat grow harder, still survive.
And what can wither – this crowd of shabby ghosts.
Where can I meet you, where do you live?

The ringing and the drumming loud bazaar,
Ringing with brightness and with reeling cries –
All inaccessibly displayed and lost –
Locks a forbidden room. At the heart of the world,
Immovable though all the planets fall,
The centre castle of universal ways,
Wearing a wild-flower garland You are reclining
And laugh and talk like a child, playing at dice.

Blood laughing in a glass of diamond.

LEWIS THOMPSON

POISON

Catching my shadow at a falter turn,
I see I spend as if I feared, in sweetness,
A poison bitter, signal, from a speechless urn.

A poison like the light that sharpens fangs—
Dense like the bound of a black tiger, war
Hollowing a midnight where no tarn or star sings.

A skull of brittle rock whose needles fester
Immortally in issue without end
Diamond through history dodged on waves of love and
                                                    murder.

Black schist, coal of dead stars, oracular stone
Ruling the desert with a cult of winds;
Granule of fever that flutes thin, disbands the bone.

This regal medicine, eating every glass,
Who then can use ?—the Taoist wizard or
Egyptian priest who ride the buffalo, the ass.

—Who ride on Death and Lust and ride them backward:
Shamed, shameless, they enter a capital not Caesar's:
Of one impregnable crystal, Joy, its towers and bulwarks.

LEWIS THOMPSON

THE ETERNAL MAN

   The Dionysiac frenzy
In which the world runs down,
The brotherhood of Saint and Faun,
Wisdom and Folly, Sun and Moon,
I celebrate, remembering
Rasputin in the moonlit wood,
That antinomian ecstasy,
Byzantine Bacchus he adored—
Winebibber, glutton, friend of whores.

   The cup of anguish, desert bread;
The forgiven adulteress,
Her perfume on that homeless head;
The beloved, the betrayer's kiss;
Gold, myrrh received, repelled;
The scourge and whip of cords;
The rod and bitter crown,
Nails and mouth-twisting vinegar—
All that contrived self-suffering,
Guilt, wrong and blasphemy,
The natural fig-tree cursed.

   Did they with more than lunatic
Imagination, subtlety
Redeem, betray, annul
All law and prophecy ?
Did the Sole Actor, the One Fate,
Play out the last of love and thought ?
Did he but calm life-water lashed
With cosmic winds of fantasy—
The glittering quicksilver sea

Those cold volcanoes rule?

Sun dark and moon like blood,
Pure faith and raging mockery,
Shadow that tortured head,
The lost, tormented, Saint's, Magician's heart—
Apollo, Judas, Faust and Pharisee.
At midnight, at the bridegroom's secret hour,
The foolish virgin's morning of despair
What pure, what loud and all-revealing cry
Won beyond God and every heaven or hell ?

Before and after good and ill,
All life and death—alone
And nude, behold the Son of Man—
Adam at last self-known,
Equal at last to his glory and misery—
Wisdom and Folly wed
Passion and Peace, pure Love and Wantonness—
By this one timeless Moment, this
'Pulsation of the Artery'
(Osiris dead, Adonis crowned,
Odin hung bleeding from the tree)
Magic and myth and history undone—
All prophecy fulfilled, and re-begun.

For from the hideous, hollow heart of Man
Wandering self-lost, in pitiful loves, alone,
'Those branches of the night and day'
The sun and moon, heaven and hell are sprung.
His lover Shah Lateef as heard God say:
'Man is my secret, I am his'.
Blake, the great Chandidas

Knew, loved and sang
That root of all the gods, all heresies—
'Listen, O brother man:
There is no Truth
Beyond, higher than Man'.

LEWIS THOMPSON

DAVID GASCOYNE

TENEBRAE

Brown darkness on the gazing face
In the cavern of candlelight reflects
The passing of the immaterial world in the deep eyes.

The granite organ in the crypt
Resounds with rising thunder through the blood,
With daylight song, unearthly song that floods
The brain with bursting suns:
Yet it is night.

It is the endless night, whose very star
Is in the spirit like the snow of dawn,
Whose meteors are the brilliance of summer,
And whose wind and rain
Are all the halcyon freshness of the valley rivers,
Where the swans,
White, white in the light of dream,
Still dip their heads.

Clear night !
He has no need of candles who can see
A longer, more celestial day than ours.

DE PROFUNDIS

Out of these depths:

Where footsteps wander in the marsh of death and an
Intense infernal glare is on our faces facing down:

Out of these depths, what shamefaced cry
Half choked in the dry throat, as though a stone
Were our confounded tongue, can ever rise:
Because the mind has been struck blind
And may no more conceive
Thy Throne…

Because the depths
Are clear with only death's
Marsh-light, because the rock of grief
Is clearly too extreme for us to breach:
Deepen our depths,

And aid our unbelief.

DAVID GASCOYNE

KYRIE

Is man's destructive lust insatiable ? There is
Grief in the blow that shatters the innocent face.
Pain blots out the clearer sense. And pleasure suffers
The trial thrust of death even in the bride's embrace.

The black catastrophe that can lay waste our worlds
May be unconsciously desired. Fear masks our face;
And tears as warm and cruelly wrung as blood
Are tumbling even in the mouth of our grimace.

How can our hope ring true ? fatality of guilt
And complicated anguish confounds time and place;
While from the tottering ancestral house an angry voice
Resounds in prophecy. Grant us extraordinary grace,

O spirit hidden in the dark in us and deep,
And bring to light the dream out of our sleep.

DAVID GASCOYNE

CAVATINA

Now we must bear the final real
Convulsion of the breast, for the sublime
Relief of the catharsis; and the cruel
Clear grief; the dear redemption from the crime
The sublimation of the evil dream.

Beneath, all is confused, dense and impure:
Extraordinary shiftings of a nameless mass
From plane to plane, then some obscure
Catastrophe:
               The shattered Cross
High on its storm-lit hill, the searchlight eyes
Whose lines divide the black dome of the skies,
Are implicated; and the Universe of Death —
Gold, excrement and flesh, the spirit's malady,
A secret animal's hot breath…

Yet through disaster a faint melody
Insists; and the interior suffering like a silver wire
Enduring and resplendent, strongly plied
By genius' hands into the searching fire
At last emerges and is purified.

Its force like violins in pure lament
Persists, sending ascending stairs
Across the far wastes of the firmament
To carry starwards all our weight of tears.

DAVID GASCOYNE

REX MUNDI

I heard a herald's note announce the coming of a king.

He who came sounding his approach was a small boy;
The household trumpet that he flourished a tin toy.

Then from a bench beneath the boughs that lately Spring
Had hung again with green across the avenue, I rose
To render to the king who came the subjects honour owe.

And as I waited, wondered why it was that such a few
Were standing there with me to see him pass; but
                                        understood
As soon as he came into sight, this was a monarch no
Crowds of this world can recognize, to hail him as they
                                        should.

He drove past in a carriage that was drawn by a white goat;
King of the world to come where all shall be now is new,
Calmy he gazed on our pretentious present that is not.

Of morals, classes, business, war, this child
Knew nothing. We were pardoned when he smiled.

If you hear it in the distance, do not scorn the herald's note.

DAVID GASCOYNE

REMEMBERING THE DEAD

In the mornings, the day-labourers must set to work once
more, and daily tasks be newly undertaken or resumed; and
they who work must disregard their usual disillusionment.

'We shall not see a culmination of these labours; our handiwork
will not last long nor our success outlive us; our successors
taking over what we've done will as like as not disparage it; and
if we build houses, they are for strangers to live in or for the
next War to destroy.
    Meanwhile we will lose ourselves with a will in what we do
today. We will tacitly discourage those who would recall too
many things or pay too much attention to the future. (All that
we cannot see is very small and unimportant). We will put guilt
upon them and they shall be silenced'.

And in the mornings, nevertheless, in such a year as this when
rain has early in the season put an end to all hope of another
extravagant summer (since a year or two ago an unexpectedly
Elysian climate did for once transform the country with such
profusion and intensity of flower-hues and foliage that for the
first time many millions were amazed by the earth's
magnificence); on wet summer mornings, when electric light
has to be turned on in the offices in the City, and listlessness
and resignation walk the streets, some of the workers (no-one
knows how many but they may be very numerous) are disturbed
by thoughts they have not thought themselves, distracted at
their work as though by voices from beneath the chilly ground.

Think, ah! Think how vastly they outnumber us by now, the
populations of the underworld ! How immemorially have they
been accumulating there, and how enormous must their

number be whom there are none now living to remember. Think how they too may all be working.

I think they think of us — Oh, how incalculably more than we ever think of them! We scarcely think of them at all; we all prefer soon to forget; if we remember, it is only with regret. They think of us, they think of all of us; they think critically, no doubt, perhaps constructively, with more understanding than we have. Perhaps all day, all night uninterruptedly.

It may be that only they fully realize that there is no other way of solving the problems of life and death than by thinking about them always.

We do not know the whole Truth; we think we know the truth. We cannot know it, yet we must. We must seek the Truth we do not know, nor can know while we are still searchers here. Those who have neither curiosity nor doubts are the only real dead.

DAVID GASCOYNE

KATHLEEN RAINE

FROM THE HOLLOW HILL

One night in a dream
The poet who had died a year ago
Led me up the ancient stair
Of an ancestral tower of stone.
Towards us out of the dark blew such sweet air
It was the warmth of the spirit, I knew,
Fragrant with wild thyme that grew
In childhood's fields; he led me on
Touched a thin partition, and was gone.
Beyond the fallen barrier
Bright over sweet meadows rose the sun.

FROM ON A DESERTED SHORE

In heart's truth I declare
What most I fear
To find beyond death's veil:
Not legendary hells of ice and fire
But a face too merciful
For my own devil-peopled soul to bear.

KATHLEEN RAINE

I HAD MEANT TO WRITE...

I had meant to write a different poem,
But, pausing for a moment in my unweeded garden,
Noticed, all at once, paradise descending in the morning sun
Filtered through leaves.
Enlightening the meagre London ground, touching with
                                            green
Transparency the cells of life.
The blackbird hopped down, robin and sparrow came,
And the thrush, whose nest is hidden
Somewhere, it must be, among invading buildings
Whose walls close in,
But for the garden birds inexhaustible living waters
Fill a stone basin from a garden hose.

I think, it will soon be time
To return to the house, to the day's occupation,
But here, time neither comes or goes.
The birds do not hurry away, their day
Neither begins nor ends.
Why can I not stay ? Why leave
Here, where it is always,
And time leads only away
From this hidden ever-present simple place.

KATHLEEN RAINE

THE PRESENCE

Present, ever-present presence,
Never have you not been
Here and now in every now and here,
And still you bring
From your treasury of colour, of light,
Of scents, notes, the evening blackbird's song,
How clear among the green and fragrant leaves,
As in childhood always new, anew.
My hand that writes is ageing, but I too
Repeat only and again
The one human song, from memory
Of a joy, a mode
Not I but the music knows
That forms, informs us, utters with our voices
Concord of heaven and earth, of high and low, who are
That music of the spheres Pythagoras heard.
I, living, utter as the blackbird
In ignorance of what it tells, the undying voice.

KATHLEEN RAINE

MILLENNIAL HYMN TO THE LORD SHIVA

1.

Earth no longer
Hymns the Creator,
The seven days of wonder,
The Garden is over —
All the stories are told,
The seven seals broken
All that begins
Must have its ending,
Our striving, desiring,
Our living and dying,
For Time, the bringer
Of abundant days
Is Time the destroyer —
  In the Iron Age
  The Kali Yuga
  To whom can we pray
  At the end of an era
  But the Lord Shiva
  The liberator, the purifier ?

2.

Our forests are felled,
Our mountains eroded,
The wild places
Where the beautiful animals
Fond food and sanctuary
We have desolated,

A third of our seas
A third of our rivers
We have polluted
And the sea creatures dying.
Our civilization's
Blind progress
In wrong courses
Through wrong choices
Has brought us to nightmare
Where what seems,
Is, to the dreamer,
The collective mind
Of the twentieth century—
This world of wonders
Not divine creation
But a big bang
Of blind chance,
Purposeless accident,
Mother Earth's children,
Their living and loving,
Their delight in being
Not joy but chemistry,
Stimulus, reflex,
Valueless, meaningless,
While to our machines
We impute intelligence,
In computers and robots
We store information
And call it knowledge,
We seek guidance
By dialing numbers,
Pressing buttons,
Throwing switches

In place of family
Our computers are shadows,
Cast on a screen,
Bodiless voices, fleshless faces,
Where was the garden
A Disneyland
Of virtual reality,
In place of angels
The human imagination
Is peopled with footballers,
Film stars, media men,
Experts, know-all
Television personalities
Animated puppets
With cartoon faces —
    To whom can we pray
    For release from illusion,
    From the world-cave,
    But Time, the destroyer,
    The liberator, the purifier ?

    3.

The curse of Midas,
Has changed at a touch,
A golden hand shake
Earthly paradise
To lifeless matter,
Where once was seed-time,
Summer, and Winter
Food-chain, factory farming,
Monocrops for supermarkets,
Pesticides, weed killers

Birdless springs
Endangered species,
Battery-hens, hormone injections
Artificial insemination,
Implants, transplants, sterilization,
Surrogate births, contraception,
Cloning, genetic engineering, abortion,
And our days shall be short
In the land we have sown
With the Dragon's teeth
Where armies arise
Fully armed on our killing-fields,
With land-mines and missiles,
Tanks and artillery,
Gasmasks and body-bags,
Our aircraft rain down
Fire and destruction
Pour spacecraft broadcast
Lies and corruption,
Our elected parliaments
Parrot their rhetoric
Of peace and democracy
While the truth we deny
Returns in our dreams
Of Armageddon,
The death-wish, the arms-trade,
Hatred and slaughter
Profitable employment
Of our thriving cities,
The arms-race
To the end of the world
Of our post-modern, post-Christian,
Post-human nations,

Progress to the nihil
Of our spent civilization
But cause and effect,
Just and inexorable
Law of the universe
No fix of science,
Nor amenable god
Can save us from ourselves
The selves we have become,
We are all in it,
No one is blameless—
   At the end of history
   To who can we pray
   But to the destroyer,
   The liberator, the purifier ?

     4.

But great is the realm
Of the world-creator,
The world-sustainer
From whom we come
In whom we move
And have our being
About us, within us
The wonders of wisdom,
The trees and the fountains,
The stars and the mountains,
All the children of joy,
The loved and the known,
The unknowable mystery
To whom we return
Through the world-destroyer—

Holy, holy
At the end of the world
The purging fire
Of the purifier, the liberator !

KATHLEEN RAINE

WILLIAM STAFFORD

CLIMBING ALONG THE RIVER

Willows never forget how it feels
to be young.

Do you remember where you came from?
Gravel remembers.

Even the upper end of the river
believes in the ocean.

Exactly at midnight
yesterday sighs away.

What I believe is,
all animals have one soul.

Over the land they love
they crisscross forever.

WHEN I MET MY MUSE

I glanced at her and took my glasses
off — they were still singing. They buzzed
like a locust on the coffee table and then
ceased. Her voice belled forth, and the
sunlight bent. I felt the ceiling arch, and
knew that nails up there took a new grip
on whatever they touched. "I am your own
way of looking at things," she said. "When
you allow me to live with you, every
glance at the world around you will be
a sort of salvation." And I took her hand.

WILLIAM STAFFORD

EARTH DWELLER

It was all the clods at once become
precious; it was the barn, and the shed,
and the windmill, my hands, the crack
Arlie made in the ax handle: oh, let me stay
here humbly, forgotten, to rejoice in it all;
let the sun casually rise and set.
If I have not found the right place,
teach me; for somewhere inside, the clods are
vaulted mansions, lines through the barn sing
for the saints forever, the shed and windmill
rear so glorious the sun shudders like a gong.

Now I know why people worship, carry around
magic emblems, wake up talking dreams
they teach to their children: the world speaks.
The world speaks everything to us.
It is our only friend.

WILLIAM STAFFORD

ENTERING HISTORY

Remember the line in the sand?
You were there, on the telly, part of
the military. You didn't want to
give it but they took your money
for those lethal tanks and the bombs.

Minorities, they don't have a country
even if they vote: "Thanks, anyway,"
the majority says, and you are left there
staring at the sand and the line they drew,
calling it a challenge, calling it "ours."

Where was your money when the tanks
grumbled past? Which bombs did you buy
for the death rain that fell? Which year's
taxes put that fire to the town
where the screaming began?

WILLIAM STAFFORD

SECURITY

Tomorrow will have an island. Before night
I always find it. Then on to the next island.
These places hidden in the day separate
and come forward if you beckon.
But you have to know they are there before they exist.

Some time there will be a tomorrow without any island.
So far, I haven't let that happen, but after
I'm gone others may become faithless and careless.
Before them will tumble the wide unbroken sea,
and without any hope they will stare at the horizon.

So to you, Friend, I confide my secret:
to be a discoverer you hold close whatever
you find, and after a while you decide
what it is. Then, secure in where you have been,
you turn to the open sea and let go.

WILLIAM STAFFORD

MERMAID

Watery light from deeps of submarine time
streamed fluttering around her in air
when the fisherman lifted her
out of his net;
slowly on land her silver faded,
her strangeness made safe now,
baptized and married
learning human words.

The ripe moon hangs
like a lamp
in blind man's country
as clothed in matronly black the mermaid wanders
even by tideless pond and puddle
seeking the impassable way
back to her lost & simple immortality.

FROM CUMAE

Should the wandering holy isle appear,
& dead sun-gods move about our skies
who are now but sunburnt dust in Pyramid City,
an invisible moon will reverse time's buried tides,
our ever-falling tower
                    hang motionless on the wind,
and Hades fear for his unconquered rule,
the King of Castle Mortal.

SALLY PURCELL

LOQUITOR SPIRITUS

Thirty nine primary colours, in our world,
are shaken from the sun.

What you read as nightmare, in webs of mist,
shadows of a roaring wind
or scribble on a yellowhammer's egg,
is to us clear message & password.

White roots threading round cracked bone
Draw your last design—
Immortal, golden, our unfallen tree.

SALLY PURCELL

PYTHIA

Outside, in the sun, bees & blue flowers
grow in flaking sarcophagi.
Humanity's house full of mirrors & bells
has no song for one, Apollo's oracle
who speaks with dead men & daimons
in their cavern of mist and fear, for she,
drawing her nature from both kingdoms,
has chosen the black solstice underground.

SALLY PURCELL

ONE WING-BEAT OF THE HEART CAN HOLD

One wing-beat of the heart can hold
centuries, heights of a third heaven,
a stumble in a dream, a waking
lost in a small familiar field
within sight of the lights of home.

SALLY PURCELL

EASTER '87

Man imagines escaping at last
from the kingdom of idols,
but the tracks lead again and again
back to the ivory gate.

Ash & salt & quiet sand
petrify one rippling
meadow after another;
a sickness devours the stone.

Healing light overflows from an empty grave;
God's body is a crystal; whole or broken,
every part of the crystal is full of sun.

SALLY PURCELL

THE TIMELESSNESS OF BEING IN LOVE

The timelessness of being in love
brings closer
lands never wholly lost
beneath that bitter wave,

    alchemically transformed
    into time aorist.

SALLY PURCELL

LOVE POEM IN TWOS AND THREES

What kind of people
are these? Some stammer
of land, some
want nothing but light—
no house or land
thrown away for a woman,
no ample recklessness.
How much I need
a woman's soul, felt
in my own knees,
shoulders and hands.
I was born sad!
I am a northern goat
of winter light,
up to my knees in snow.
Standing by you, I am
glad as the clams
at high tide, eerily
content as the amorous
ocean owls.

THE INDIGO BUNTING

I go to the door often.
Night and summer. Crickets
Lift their cries.
I know you are out.
You are driving
Late through the summer night.

I do not know what will happen.
I have no claim on you.
I am one star
You have as guide; others
Love you, the night
So dark over the Azores.

You have been working outdoors,
Gone all week. I feel you
In this lamp lit
So late. As I reach for it
I feel myself
Driving through the night.

I love a firmness in you
That disdains the trivial
And regains the difficult.
You become part then
Of the firmness of night,
The granite holding up walls.

There were women in Egypt who
Supported with their firmness the stars

As they revolved,
Hardly aware
Of the passage from night
To day and back to night.

I love you where you go
Through the night, not swerving,
Clear as the indigo
Bunting in her flight,
Passing over two
Thousand miles of ocean.

ROBERT BLY

IN THE MONTH OF MAY

In the month of May, when all leaves open,
I see when I walk how well all things
Lean on each other, how the bees work,
The fish make their living the first day.
Monarchs fly high; then I understand
I love you with what in me is unfinished.

I love you with what in me is still
Changing, what has no head or arms
Or legs, what has not found its body.
And why shouldn't the miraculous,
Caught on this earth, visit
The old man alone in his hut?

And why shouldn't Gabriel, who loves honey,
Be fed with our own radishes and walnuts?
And lovers, tough ones, how many there are
Whose holy bodies are not yet born.
Along the roads, I see so many places
I would like us to spend the night.

ROBERT BLY

ADVICE FROM THE GEESE

Hurry ! The world is not going to get better,
Do what you want to do now. The prologue is over.
Soon actors will come onstage carrying the coffin.

I don't want to frighten you, but not a stitch can be taken
On your quilt unless you study. The geese will tell you—
A lot of crying goes on before dawn comes.

Do you have a friend who has studied prisons ?
Does a friend say 'I love the twelve houses' ?
The word 'houses' suggests prisons all by itself.

So much suffering goes on among prisoners.
There is so much grief in the cells. So many bolts
Of lightning keep coming from the unborn.

Please don't expect that the next President
Will be better than this one. Four o' clock
In the morning is the time to read Basilides.

Every seed spends many nights in the earth.
Give up the idea the world will get better by itself.
You will not be forgiven if you refuse to study.

ROBERT BLY

A GLIMPSE OF AMERICAN HISTORY

If we go back, if we walk into the old darkness, we will find
Washington brooding under the long bridges,
The dead still ablaze in the anguish of the egg,
Screams reverberating in the compression chamber of
                                                      shells,
Soldiers that disappear into the tunnels inside the flashlight,
Sioux bodies falling and soap buried alive.

Sugar beets that give blood migrate to the stars,
Drunken ward-heelers crawl in the icy gutters.
Our history is the story of something that failed:
A greedy fire is burning on our fingertips,
Fingers that turn over pages of deeds, fingers on fire,
Fingers that would light the sky if lifted at night.

                                                ROBERT BLY

THE PELICANS AT WHITE HORSE KEY

Occasionally spreading their wings to the sun, pelicans
Dive for fish from dawn to dusk. The Lord of this World
Is a painter working at night in a dark room.

Earth is the place where we've agreed to throw
Away the gifts Adam's grandfather gave us
During the dark time before eternity was born.

The lover's body belongs to ruined earth.
The scattered stars belong to the Milky Way.
The potato field belongs to early night.

The Monitor Lizard is a child of the Mother,
And a favourite child. The Monitor holds a snake
Immobile for an hour and then eats.

We know it's not good to have sharp opinions;
But would you think so much of Noah
If he had thrown away his bag of nails ?

Four times this month I have dreamt I am
A murderer; and I am. These lines are paper boats
Set out to float on the sea of repentance.

ROBERT BLY

THE TAR SAYS IT WILL ALL END BADLY

It is sadness, all right. It starts again. Another man
Walking underneath the ladder of his voice. Now he's under
                                        the mountain
Where his voice is in prison. There is no way out.

So my feelings are burned again. The tar is counting
Up my defeats again. The master of the tar
Says that all this will end badly!

You can see the heavy blankets hanging down
From the widow's bed. You and I
Are horses hurrying at night over the snow-covered fields.

For three days all you have felt is the worthlessness
And insufficiencies of your childhood. Many of the roads
                                        are blocked
Tonight, and the sense of being defeated is returning.

How foolish it is of us to imagine that we can
Ever be happy like the others! Some curse was laid on us,
Like those old drunkards who get lost on the way home.

Robert, it's amazing that you have been
Published at all. The tar says that we are all
In heaven, and everything has to be paid for.

                                        ROBERT BLY

BROODING ON DISAPPEARANCE

Why was Mohammed so faithful to his wife?
Why did so many die in the Second World War?
Why do some love affairs resemble a blow of lightning?

Low notes in music bring us close to weeping.
We remember what happened to us before birth.
Our unease can also be a form of faithfulness.

Tell me why the sleeper dreams of crimes
He has never committed, why the child cries, and why
The dreamer visits other continents by night.

A lot of disappointment enters into every birth.
People say that even in the highest heavens
Men and women about to be reborn are weeping.

We are all graduate students of disappearance.
We have been born and have died so many times.
You'll never be able to get a straight answer from us.

Millions of people have been born before us.
They didn't bother to tell us what happened.
We keep trying to remember the rest of the story.

ROBERT BLY

ANDREW HARVEY

KABIR:

'TRUE KNOWLEDGE'

This, I've discovered, is true knowledge—
Those who scramble to get into a boat
Sink like a stone midstream,
While the shelterless and abandoned
Reach the other shore,
Those who dare to take
The hard, winding, thorny road
Get to town in the end;
Those who stroll the easy highway
Get robbed or even killed
Soon after they set out.
Everyone's wound in illusion's web—
The so-called "holy" as much as the worldly,
And those who run for safety
Under the comforting dais
Of form and ritual and dogma—
Well, life's hurricane lashes them.
Stay out in the open:
You'll be left safe and dry.
The ones Love never savages
Live in boredom and pain;
Those Love devours like a cannibal
Live in bliss forever.
The ones who lose their own eyes
Come to see the whole Creation
Blazing in their own Light;

Those who hold on to their sight
Remain blind as bats in full noon.
When I began to awake to Truth
I saw how bizarre and crazy the world really is!

TRANSLATED BY ANDREW HARVEY

'DON'T BOAST'

Kabir, don't boast about your body,
That skin-sheet stuffed with bones;
Princes who rode regal stallions
Under umbrellas of gold
Now lie folded in earth.

Kabir, don't boast
about your gorgeous palaces;
Today or tomorrow
The ground will be your bed
And grass smother your head.

Don't boast about your luck, Kabir,
And despise the desperate:
Your ship's still out at sea—
Who knows its fate?

Kabir don't boast
Of your beauty and youth:
Today or tomorrow
You'll have to abandon them
Like a serpent its own skin.

TRANSLATED BY ANDREW HARVEY

'THOSE WHO KNOW'

Those who know
The million million colors and forms
Spring from one color, one form,
Pay no attention whatsoever
To castes or divisions.

Those who do not recognize God
Die;
Those who give their hearts
To anything but God
Die;
Those who enthuse about the Scriptures
They die too —
They adore the words
But never realize
The Spirit behind them.

All they go about doing in fact,
Is applying makeup
To eyes already blind with prejudice —
O Sheikh Tazi, realize
Once and for all
The Lord of Eternity lives
In every pot.

TRANSLATED BY ANDREW HARVEY

'THE BELOVED IS IN ME'

The Beloved is in me, and the Beloved is in you,
As life is hidden in every seed,
So rubble your pride, my friend,
And look for Him within you.

When I sit in the heart of His world
A million suns blaze with light,
A burning blue sea spreads across the sky,
Life's turmoil falls quiet,
All the stains of suffering wash away

Listen to the unstruck bells and drums!
Love is here; plunge into its rapture!
Rains pour down without water;
Rivers are streams of light.

How could I ever express
How blessed I feel
To revel in such vast ecstasy
In my own body?

This is the music
Of soul and soul meeting,
Of the forgetting of all grief.
This is the music
That transcends all coming and going.

TRANSLATED BY ANDREW HARVEY

RUMI:

'DRAW IT NOW FROM ETERNITY'S JAR'

Come, come, awaken all true drunkards!
Pour the wine that is Life itself!
O cupbearer of the Eternal Wine,
Draw it now from Eternity's Jar!
This wine doesn't run down the throat
But it looses torrents of words!
Cupbearer, make my soul fragrant as musk,
This noble soul of mine that knows the Invisible!
Pour out the wine for the morning drinkers!
Pour them this subtle and priceless musk!
Pass it around to everyone in the assembly
In the cups of your blazing drunken eyes!
Pass a philter from your eyes to everyone else's
In a way the mouth knows nothing of,
For this is the way cupbearers always offer
The holy and mysterious wine to lovers.
Hurry, the eyes of every atom in Creation
Are famished for this flaming-out of splendor!
Procure for yourself this fragrance of musk
And with it split open the breast of heaven!
The waves of the fragrance of this musk
Drive all Josephs out of their minds forever!

TRANSLATED BY ANDREW HARVEY

'WHAT REMAINS BUT DROWNING?'

Love does not live in science and learning
Or in any careful order of pages and letters.
Whatever people chatter about
Is not the Way of Lovers.
The branches of Love are in pre-eternity
Its roots in the post-eternal.
This is a Tree that does not exist
On any supports of heaven or earth.
We have dethroned reason and imprisoned desire,
For the majesty of Divine Love
Cannot live with such fools and their habits.
So long as you hunger after anything,
What you long for will be an idol.
When Love decides to love you back
You will no longer exist.
All sailors totter on planks of fear and hope—
But when "planks" and "sailor" have vanished,
What remains but drowning?
Shams of Tabriz, you are sea and pearl;
The mystery of your being
Is the secret of the Creator.
My Soul, the first time I saw you
My soul heard wonders from your soul.
And when my heart drank water from your fountain
It drowned in you and the river swept me away.

TRANSLATED BY ANDREW HARVEY

'THE MASTER OF THE WORK'

The grapes of my body can only become wine
After the winemaker tramples me.
Surrender my spirit like grapes to his trampling
So my inmost heart can laze and dance with joy.
"I cannot bear any more anguish, any more cruelty!"
The trampler stuffs cotton in his ears: "I am not
                working in ignorance.
You can deny me if you want, you have every excuse,
But it is I who am the Master of this Work.
And when through my Passion you reach Perfection,
You will never be done praising my name."

TRANSLATED BY ANDREW HARVEY

'GRACE IS THE DOOR'

Cupbearer, pour the wine! Let it flow and keep flowing!
I am sick of swinging between hope and fear.
Shatter thought, I want nothing to do with it!
Tear from my heart all unstable imaginings!
Hack from their chains the shameless joys of passion!
Dance into our assembly, Beloved, unveil Your Face,
Scatter graces with each swirl of Your robe of flame.
Look at these madmen dancing out of themselves for You:
See how they've stripped themselves of the rags of time!
Even to detachment the heart can be attached, God knows,
For the heart is a net spread for misery.
Transform my heart to a placeless place of safety,
Carry it to the mountains where it dies into You.
Come quickly! My body's tired of this country;
Make it drunk, set it free, call to it, "Come quickly!"
Offer me a cup overflowing with the wine of wonder
So I can no longer tell my head from my feet.
Don't give me bread, or water, or peace, or sleep;
Thirst for You is blood-money for a hundred souls like mine.
Today, my beloved, you have swept me to Your table
Let me stammer and stagger at the Glory of Your Feast.
News has raced through the city: Today's the Day of Joy!
You are an ass if you want anything but God,
A sad and crazy ass trying to get fat on ash;
Know that the grass of ash dirties the mouth that eats it.
Remember, always, what Mohammed said:
"Stay away from the green of filthy places!"
Beloved, I am far from the grass of the ashpits
I am far from the houris of the gardens
I am far from pride, far from vanity;

I am drunk on the wine of the Divine Majesty.
The thought of a final Beauty leaps like a deer in my heart
Like the moon racing up the sky, like a lily
Lifting its head suddenly from the river grass.
See, all the world's images are running to Your Image
Scraps of iron drawn by a magnet of light.
Diamond becomes stone before You, lions small flowers;
The sun before You shrinks tinier than any atom.
In You, this whole world blazes now like Mount Sinai,
Each of its atoms foams over with fire-water
Each soul becomes Moses lost in the Vision of God.
Each creature is soldered to You and its own Origin,
Laughing at Nothingness and clapping its own miracle.
Each leaf opens fresh and bright, each atom sings its discovery:
"Surrender is the key to happiness,
Grace is the door to the peace beyond the mind."

TRANSLATED BY ANDREW HARVEY

SEEKERS

Each of us is searching for
a wise man or woman
to lead us,
to present us
a scroll heavy with answers.

Some of us have climbed the mountain,
tracked the glacier's crust,
lain down in snow for days, years,
burning away to essence,
preparing.

Others have clung
to the underside of overhanging rock
until their fingers turned
to stone,
until they were riveted
like lead
to this thin edge of certainty.

And others wander, drifting like mist
through the valleys.

What is it we are seeking?
What will we do if we are brushed
by this lion's mane ?

A CLOTH OF FINE GOLD

You may think
that first lit flame
was the ultimate blaze,
the holy fire revealed.

What do you know
of furnaces?
This is a sun that returns
again and again, refining, igniting,
pouring your spirit
through a cloth of delicate gold
until all dross is taken
and you are sweet as
clarified butter
in god/the goddess' mouth.

DOROTHY WALTERS

THE SUPPLICANTS

"At the throne of God, the angels have no form at all, but come as pure, raw energy..."
  Sophy Burnham

There are many ways
of approaching the throne.

Some move solemnly,
majestically,
a procession of wisemen
contemplating a final reality.

For others, it is a celebration
of the soul in love trance.
They are caught in a
fiery transformation,
a dancing beyond the reach
of silence or the Word.

Others quietly abase themselves,
moving forward slowly, intent,
imprinting the dust
again and again
with their bodies' thin shadows
as they go.

DOROTHY WALTERS

LIKE FLOWERS THAT BLOOM AT MIDNIGHT

I know all about
living in caves
with candles and scented prayers,
crossing the desert which never ends
seeking the One who is always near,
spreading my deerskin
in the forest depths
where the spirits of the blue bodied gods
hang like shadows of watching birds.

With the others, I wove
a story of connection,
something mysterious and inscrutable
we called to appear
with our fires and recitations
our songs of supplication and praise . . .
a voice spoke through us
as we chanted our words
and the centuries passed.

This time I came in other guise.
I roamed the avenues,
mingled in the market
with the restless crowds,
watched and listened in alarm
as the world reeled and
spun down
toward its approaching dark.

And I saw that this
was the time
to take on new knowledge,

move through different space,
hear with unfamiliar ears,
speak with strengthened voice,
atoms transfigured,
senses restrung,
it is happening to us all,
blazing illumination,
beauty erupting in the midst of despair,
splendor unveiled
on a field of pain,
we are being filled with light
we do not comprehend
lifted toward essence
assaulted by nameless love
at this juncture
of the finalities,
intersection of the unimaginables . . .
this is why we came.

DOROTHY WALTERS

WHO WENT UNHEARD

I think again and again
of those who went
so long unheard,
or even ignored.

Vivaldi and the children,
some hardly bigger
than their instruments.
Nobody really noticed.
No one really cared.
Yet they played on.

And dear Emily,
her letter to the world—
something kept her writing,
packets bound together in wool,
poems in mittens,
dropped for passing school children.

And of course Mozart,
his reward
the pauper's grave.
Who knows where he
entered earth?
All transmuted
to sound.

And even Bach,
out of favor at the end.

One likes to believe
that in the elsewhere realm
these were at last were fully heard,
vibrant chords circulating among
the angelic choirs,
choruses of Gloria
and string quartets
and the audience ravished — silent
becoming only this.

DOROTHY WALTERS

BEFORE

"Before I was named I belonged to you."
— *Rilke*

Wherever I was, hidden in your thigh,
a sycamore seed waiting
in earth,
a thought preparing to leap forth,
I had no name.
My body had no shape.
My eyes were not yet
opened.
Even my face was dark.
What are the features
of that which does not exist?
Nonetheless, I was yours,
an unmarked impulse,
a treasure you carried
like a charm
hung from your vest,
before you sent me
down.

DOROTHY WALTERS

WHO YOU ARE

How the body is put together,
with its tender fastenings,
its mysterious openings,
its muscles working in
smooth coordination
to convey it
where it wishes to go,
how it changes
from year to year,
from day to day,
its cells working in collusion
to carry it always
into a new configuration,
how the face communicates
its signals
wherever it goes,
whether it is
happy or sad
or puzzled
or plotting,
how the inner and outer,
organs and coverings are part
of the same being,
the same oneness
that is bound together
to make the unique creation,
the one combination
that is you,
present here, now,
spirit's abode,
soul's habitation.

never to be encountered
again in time's endless cycles.

DOROTHY WALTERS

JENI COUZYN

THE COMING OF THE ANGEL

I have seen the angel of life.
It stood all night at the foot of our bed
on the twelfth night of your life
when you were in danger.
I tell you this, Tarot Ishtar,
not to embellish your life
but so one day you will know again
what you know with such
authority now — radiance
clothed in a child.

Three times I woke and saw your angel
with my eyes, light without face
eyes without eyes
watching over us. A presence
so total
I was utterly known, safe from all harm
in the power of its love.

In the years before your dawning,
in crisis,
a being came to me as I slept
that I knew as death.
A hood of absence
a greyness that runs to the bone
stood over me, watching
till I fell from sleep
and repelled it with my terror.

Now it has returned
and because of you, love
radiant in sleep in my cradle of bones
I know it at last, old enemy—
this wondrous being, this wonder.

JENI COUZYN

WE ARE RISING FROM THE SEA

We are rising from the sea.
You thought we were drowned
but under the water
we were quietly breathing
as we walked on the sea floor
and we're looking inward now
to find out where we are.

I am not what you think, sisters, no.
You have not seen my face
nor used my true name.
I have one though — sacred
difficult to speak
difficult to hold.

It changes every moment.
It is your name also.
Learn it. Say it with me.

JENI COUZYN

from IN THE SKINHOUSE

I am clinging to the strings of the world
pulled this way and that.
Surrender, says the angel,
striking my knuckles with sharp pain.
I ache in my spine
and behind my eyes.
I am sick in the pit of my stomach.
The pain is in my pride and in my wanting.
Surrender, thunders the angel
within my body.
It is threading new cells
into a structure like a cathedral
and I, protesting
This is my body, mine.
I cannot see you.
I don't understand what you are doing.
Surrender, sighs the angel
a sea of sweetness that enfolds me.
Love. Surrender.

    *

Lips, speak only his word.
Breath, be his bird.
Eyes, his glance.
Body, his dance.

    *

You entered the muscles with a paring knife
like a strong old woman
peeling potatoes.

You entered the veins with a wire brush.
Because I have prepared for you all year
clearing the builder's rubble
from what I called
my house
welcome.

*

Your song in my body
is making me young.
I remember that the flesh
grows and dies to God's breath
which transcends
the law of earth.
Your song works in my body
not in time
but in the moment
as I see your love
in my mirror.

*

I wait for you
like a crazy person.
Someone offers me money.
Someone asks for money.
The wasps cover my hands
and my eyes.
They enter my mouth and my lungs.
They call it
'reality'.

*

Cool my pain!

Lift me from the fire!
I search for you everywhere
hoarse with grief
suddenly hear you
I am the fire.
I am your prayer.

*

You accuse the other
and defend yourself.
Try another way.
Become an eagle on the moor.
Become a mouse in the heather.
Be eagle and mouse at the same
time, and then become

the moor itself,
scent of the heather.
Knowing yourself,
release the other.

*

Forgiveness —
what does it mean ?
The bodies of the lovers
naked before you
the straight one and the broken
side by side, at rest
as if each slid
from the other's skin.
Hurt unpeeled
wound unsealed
that place inside you
where the stone opens

tears flow from rock.

*

This is how the universe is made.
He enters her
and love explodes into star
she fine as cell-point
he delicate as pollen
star exploding into flower.

JENI COUZYN

TUNING

Some days I feel
like a far-reaching ray
of the Sun.

Other days
like the riverbed
under a great Stream.

Other times I'm just trying
to wake up
from a deep sleep.

Or I start taking
mosquitoes
seriously—

thinking when I reach
the highest peak
everything will be perfect.

As if I'm practicing on a child's violin
when I already play
in the Symphony.

RELATIONSHIPS

Today everything is upside down.
It's all about money, machines
and keeping patriarchy afloat.

That's why I got divorced
and married supreme Consciousness,
always beautiful, good, and true.

A demanding relationship, to be sure,
but isn't every relationship?
And this one is worth it!

JANINE CANAN

IMPOSTERS

There's a world of 'poetry' here
I scorn, and after subtracting
sour grapes, scorn even more.

Who makes these so-called poems ?
Not poets !
Mechanics toying
with parts, vampires sucking blood

from words, instead of shedding it,
strangling language since they have
nothing to say or praise.

JANINE CANAN

WOMAN

I am not an aesthetic
object,
I don't really care
what color looks good

on me,
for I am what colors
the Earth most
beautifully.

my skin blends perfectly
with the sands,
my eyes flow
with the seas.

my smile blooms
with the flowers,
my light shines inseparably
with the sun.

My darkness glows
with the moon and the stars,
and when your eyes
have opened —

you will see.

JANINE CANAN

DEVI LOKA

Today I went to a gathering with a Goddess.
What Realm, where bubbles of light
and sweet chants bless all worlds.
She held me in her arms crying *Daughter*!
Now I never want to leave — this love,
this beauty, this peace.

*

In Devi Loka there is no illness.
Only sublime perfection.
Your heart is my heart
and the Cosmos throbs with Love.
And Love, I promise you, is more real
than anything.

*

Gone to Devi Loka — all the friends
SO BEAUTIFUL
Stunned — I did not expect this
DIVINE LIGHT.
Gone to Devi Loka — the goddesses
SHIMMERING.

JANINE CANAN

STARLIGHT

You are all that exists
and all that does not.

Words are gems that can become stars
in your flashing firmament.

We are diggers prospecting for rubies,
diamonds, emeralds and gold.

Divers hunting for pearls in this upside down
world of heavens and hells.

You are all that exists and does not exist.
We are diviners, learning how.

JANINE CANAN

CHARLES UPTON

from THE WARS OF LOVE

Our real fear
Is not of death:
By the testimony of every ghost
We know our mask survives it.
What we fear most truly
Is love itself.
   —because there is a trance in death.
You faint at one point, they say....
And then all fear and hunger
Are equal.

But in love,
Death only sharpens everything.
Blood grows in radiance.
Every sense is clarified,
Every faculty enlightened.
The fluted mask
Of the face is shattered.
You watch—having no longer any way
      to close your eyes—
How every cell in your body
Is exquisitely, mercilessly
Brought to birth.
Oblivion does not guard this gate
As it does the gate to the womb;
The chest is torn open,
And what rises to the eyes, black and red,
Like water rising in a broken ship
Is not sleep—it is Light. Death

Is only a precarious, temporary refuge
From a light like that.
The soul runs from tomb to tomb,
Praying for a little shelter,
Pounding on stone slabs with
    fists of air—
And how deaf they are, with their
    carved smiles,
With their beards of moss.
A blind hawk does not escape the dawn:
He suffers it. Hell
Is the measure of resistance;
A loving hand, laid on breast or shoulder
The measure of defeat.

CHARLES UPTON

from THE WARS OF LOVE

The greatest beauty
Is the beauty of the Invisible.

There's nowhere to turn
To take hold of
Or behold it.

Like a smell,
It comes from somewhere beyond directions.

You find it
By being the place
In which you've always known it.

Layla – that's just what she's like.
Her name has to be Night,
Because the light of day, unless it falls
On some mote of dust that
Thinks it has a name,
Is black as midnight.
Night is Qur'an – night
And all the stars.
The stars are the Book,
But night is the Mother of the Book.

She divests herself, when the recitation is ended;
Undoes the strings of existence
And drops it, like a robe.

When the lights went out
In the great banquet-hall
Where all the people I had ever known

Or ever would know
Were being entertained after dinner
By the two black-faced fuqara
Directing the spectacle
Of death and resurrection,

That was Her. Ever since that night
I have been a slave
Of the unseen beauty.

It is madness to cross the ocean
Looking for the ocean itself,
Madness to find a direction
That doesn't appear
On either globe or compass,
And then turn toward it deliberately;
Such things are not done.

But when night comes, and the wind drops
And the calm ocean reflects
The mazes of the stars,
Why not leave cloak of your existence
On the deck of the ship,
And dive, in your madness,
Into the glossy black water
That has carried you for fifty years
On the strict count of your breath,
And reach the Midnight Sun?

CHARLES UPTON

TIME TO STOP

Time to stop mistaking yourself
For the one who says he's you:
Saint, political theorist, new image of man,
Mouthpiece of his anonymous brothers
Bound in graveyard, locked in god-form,
Bones of his suicided teacher rotted dry
In some crevasse of the Sierras,
Still giving off their ghostly half-life....
Time to turn the mirror to the wall and
        consult the window instead,
To remember yourself in broad daylight
Matched against the shadow
Of the One who knows you're Him.

CHARLES UPTON

THE KING

Like a criminal I poached in the deer park.
Fear, excitement, danger:
The meat tasted good and the women thought well.
For years I went at it, the keepers no match
For such as I;
While the King bided his time with:
'He may settle down to honest employment.
Let him be.'
But there was no truth in me.

And then the King said:

'If it's the dark wood he wants, let him have it.
Let him range free, and we'll see what we see.'
Deep in its wild heart I made my home then,
Once I'd caught on how the game was being played.
Shelter built, and I grew in beside birds and small beasts
Till the wood seemed mine and I stopped being wary.
And I thought no more of markets and inns,
Company, shillings or wine.

Ah it was fine to be lone and free,
And who was King if not I?

But then the aspects turned.
Nights became thicker, winds had an edge;
Undergrowth tore me; eyes flitted and gleamed;
I became haggard, and storm came to rule;

Torrent on torrent, night upon day.
Shelter crashed, fire out, bed gone, knife lost.
Panic, I ran; terror, cried out; exhausted, fell down.

I woke surrounded by figures of menace
In a tight circle that pressed me and pinned.
They spoke with one voice, like a crow's, like a snare.
Said, Watched me a long time, knew I was theirs.
I was unknown to the town now and lived beyond law;
Come with them for rich pickings and powers more than human.
As they, that one, spoke, the darkness expanded
Into visions of gold, burning castles and whores.
Air about them rippled and smoked,
But I remained standing and gave them no sign.
Their hiss-words continued, became more insistent;
The circle about me started to close,
And me now crouching, turning, shrunken.
But I know a killer and I know a victim.
And who should know better than I?
So up I surged at them in desperation,
Punching and kicking, throttling and biting,
Crying a human cry, 'I'll die, I'll die, I'll rather die.'
Stink and mutter and curse and screech
From their filthy hell-forms as they turned to mist;
And I stayed clenched, with all power summoned,
Ready for worse, ready for onslaught,
But not to consort with such as they.

The marvel is what happens then. They're gone.
And who stands in stead now is Death himself.
He was not like anything; I say no more.
But I knew what he was from his cold emanation.
Fainting and standing, blood rising and falling,

I saw between me and his massive shape
My life, my soul itself, hovering and fluttering
In the stream of our breaths.
I saw I, yes I, and my heart broke in two
Like a splitting seed when I looked at the pictures
That showed me my life. What wretch had I been
That I had to see this?
Why was I not a seat by a fireside?
Why had I never tilled a field?
All my lies were there and all my thieving,
And the king's men I'd killed and . . . and . . .
Were those my children?   I didn't know.
'Sweet Jesus, what have I been?"

I fell down on the ground before that figure,
Broken and choking, beyond all repair.

I came to in a clearing in a kinder wood:
Lights, and a cross, and there the King stood.
He said: 'Stand easy, friend. Up from the ground.
That's better. You have found out now
How world is watered and how it is wasted.
That is the reason you were given to roam:
Only the free can come home.'

—But where is the serjeant and where is the lash?
—Be your own serjeant. Be your own lash.
  My Justice is just because I am the balance.
  And my Mercy is to give you a task
  Which you choose yourself when you know what the choice is
  And that the past is past.

Like the fool I was, I was just going to say

'Am I free to go now?' when he was gone.

Wiser than wise I tell you is that king of all souls.
My heart was so full my eyes brimmed over,
And I turned to trudge to'ards where the folk are
To begin my slow beginnings
Of being a man on earth.

ALAN JACKSON

THE THREE

In the depth of winter
In the dark of night
There was only one house,
Only one light.

I walked down the path,
I knocked on the door.
I do not think
I'd been there before.

Music and light,
Three smiling faces.
I was by the fire
In seven paces.

Oh what a blossom
Oh what a feel!
They showed me a seat;
I joined in their meal.

After we'd eaten
We cleared out the things;
'One of us plays,
One of us sings,

One of us dances.'
'Then I will too,'
I laughed and looked,
I'll dance with you.

The stars in the window,
The birds in the trees,
The fire in the chimney,
We were all these.

The sun in the morning,
The moon on its way,
Roses and silver,
Nothing was gray.

A rich deep blue,
A scarlet bloom,
Like living liquids,
Filled the room.

Then we sat down
And talked till dawn.
Our eyes were shining.
We could not yawn.

'Where were you going?'
'Coming to you.'
'But you didn't know.'
'Of course, I knew.

I know what is
And what is not.
I know the cold,
I know the hot

I know what quickens,
I know what kills;
I know what drains;

I know what fills

When I couldn't see
I followed my nose.
When I couldn't hear
I followed my toes.'

'Then many a bump
And many a smack
I expect you got
On such a track.'

'I certainly did.
I'm covered in bruises.'
'You're not, you know.
Who wins, loses.

You are human
And we're pleased
That you found us,
Though we teased,

But you must go
You cannot stay:
Soon it will be
Another day.

And you are called
Back to your place:
Great is the work
Of the human race.

Now, don't be sad.

You won't forget.
And we are there
In dry and wet;

In hot and cold,
Dull and shine,
In wither and bloom'
You'll see our sign.

Whenever you look
With light in your eyes
You'll almost see,
And hear our cries.'

The house was fading,
The fire was gone;
It was the earth
I was standing on.

'Goodbye goodbye,
True hearts can't fail!
Goodbye, goodbye,
Green is the trail!'

It was very cold
And rosy blue
I heard the cock
A doodle do.

I saw some smoke
And birds in trees
I heard their laughter
In the breeze.

I wasn't sad
For I understood
My friends were alive
In water and wood.

A wonderful fire
Flamed through my heart.
I'd walking to do;
I made a start.

ALAN JACKSON

JEHANNE MEHTA

'SEEK NOT TO HOLD HER'

Seek not to hold her
for she is given to the bees.

Her breasts are two
white roses
dispensing sweet nectar

and the ripening fruit
of her womb is what the world
waits for –
in the patient eyes
of her lover
and in the flaming palms
of supplicants
starving, under the Indian
sun.

Seek not to hold her
for she will give birth
among the bees, alone
in the wilderness

and when she passes
wide winged
with her precious progeny –
on the windswept soil

which has forgotten
how to weep
you will hear the
fresh dew falling.

JEHANNE MEHTA

TYMPANUM
(The troubadour)

I am not anything you give a name to,
There is nothing I am bound to do.
I stand within the circle of my freedom.
There is nowhere I am bound to go,

But if you should wish to circumscribe me,
Bend your thinking round into an O,
Stretching the finest skin across it,
Tightened like the drawn string on a bow.

I am nothing but an instrument of hearing,
A membrane, taut as ever any drum,
All senses fused together to make one.

Strike me with your name and with your beauty;
Vibrating with your pain and with your love,
I shall pierce the very stars with song.

JEHANNE MEHTA

SOIL

This black brown stuff
which I dig in I turn over
this medium of birth
which I open with a spade
this warm smelling close smelling
matrix which I open
with my fingers folding
back the green hair
covering to plant
new things in the careful
darkness trusting
that letting the seeds go
letting the swell-bellied bulbs
go, pointing up to the sky
trusting she will know
without thought, how
to deliver them
perfumed and petal folded perfect
to the opening sun

this home of the careful worm
careful of the air and space
which it brings, digests
into this substructure
this substructure which
sticks to my fingers and
darkens my fingernails
with clean loam scents

rising from her when fingered
by the frost or drummed
on by the rain, by the
rhythms of the warm October
rain, where roots move out
exploring her with eager tenderness
and strong downward direction
thrusting into heavier deeps
of clay and stone

this deep threshold
which the plants know opens
into light
empowering their roots, engendering
levity that can cause
rocks to split their sides
and crack open the man-made
roads in lines of laughter
that no concrete can stop
for long,
this home of fundamental levity and light
who gives birth upwards
to the sky through countless
green mouths, shaping syllables
which clothe her intimate darkness
in beauty which if we do not
admire we destroy by apathy:

this black brown stuff
which I dig in, turn over
this matrix which I open

with my fingers to plant
new things...
this is my body
being woman
and being woman, being she,
what to do but bear her lightness, whiteness
bear her witness
always upwards
and out, through my
green throat

JEHANNE MEHTA

SONNET

You are so far spread greater than you know:
You track the long trod dismal daily grey,
boned, kerbed and neatly boxed in a clay
border, heart blindfold, not even a toe
out of line, thinking unopened, slow,
no wild verges; yoked to the straitened day;
But at the sluice, dreams, thronging the raceway,
Heave at the wet boards, lunging for the flow.

An angel pounds at your temples, stirs your gut;
the sheer light , landing, grips you like a crown.
He cannot bear these streams diverted, channels cut,
and you to yourself dim wasteland overgrown.
Will you turn the heavy winches of this gate,
before the terrible roar of your own soul breaks it down ?

JEHANNE MEHTA

THE WAITING

The waiting is intense;
not a grass blade but knows it,
now time has come off its hinges
and opens all ways.

There is a watching,
a listening, sharp as January shoots
that pierce the patient earth,
a gathering from all four directions:
fur, feathers, and the folk
of the mounds, the stones and of the trees,
the ones we only see with closed eyes,
or imprinted for a moment on bark,
swift caught in water swirls, then gone,
dissolving into
rippling shadows.

Do we dare to be transparent,
fired by the many dimensions of love?
Do we dare to be transparent in this fire,
flame feathered like the phoenix?

For we are the beacon, the burning pillar,
a-shine with eyes,
where what was below is rerouted
to the stars,
what was lost in deep space
reconnects with the heart
of earth.

The waiting is intense;
not a grass blade but feels it,
now time has come off its hinges.

The waiting intensifies.

JEHANNE MEHTA

JENNIFER DOANE UPTON

SILENCE

Silence, you are beside me and I have to fight you, I who
   never go to the wars.
   And the wars happen all the time.
Silence, you are lying to me. You tell me lies every day. Even
   when I don't speak, you lie to me.
Silence, I have to talk to you in a weak language. I've had to
   make my language vulnerable. I wanted a strong language
   more than anything and I needed strength. It must be
that all the strength I've built up so slowly and carefully within
   myself
doesn't matter to you. You've put agony into my creative energies
   and I can't help but believe that you want to destroy me.
Silence, do you want to destroy me? You keep bringing me
   material I can't control.
When I was sick last week I vomited on the floor
   and for a whole day I was too weak to clean it up. I believe
   you caused that.
If I don't confront you then everything I say
   will be worth nothing in the world.
   To whatever it is in me that wants to destroy and kill.
   The silence is hate.
   Hate kills.
Silence, do you remember how jealous I used to be of my sister.
   I wrote a story once about a girl who hated her sister
   very much, and when the sister died, that girl
   started to become like her sister.
Silence, when my great uncle died you made him ask again and
   again for my sister,
   and never once ask for me.

JENNIFER DOANE UPTON

THE STONES OF MEN

I have looked for you in the faces
of all those people who turn backward
like the sun turning toward death
for fear of you, whom they might see.

I have asked for your whereabouts everywhere,
and every place upon this earth has been revealed to me.
I cannot hold
all I see.

Now, if I think about you at all, I hide it.
I hold my voice back in the market place
to keep from talking about you.

Today I have not met a single person who is not heartless.
I have not met a single person who does not believe
that I am already staying with you
whom I am searching for.

These are the stones given to all men and women.
Not one of us can live a single day
sitting upon this pile of stones.

JENNIFER DOANE UPTON

THE MASSACRE

Sometimes I feel that the dead
are mourning for us.
They approach when we can't see them
They talk to us when we can't hear them
and no matter how much they try to touch us,
we always forget the knowledge
that when we lost them
we also lost ourselves.

I feel within my nightmares
the cruelty they experience when they love us—
Wanting to speak to us
means wanting to have the very bodies
it has just become impossible for them to have.
We always look upon them as souls
and we say we love them with our souls—
Our bodies no longer know how to love them.

And in their own way they are cruel to us.
By the time we remember
recently forgotten names
they have already changed
and left us with the love that was rightfully ours
from the beginning.
It is only we, whose knowledge comes from our
bodily lives
who can turn their cruelty
back into tenderness.

JENNIFER DOANE UPTON

THE MEETING WITH GOD

I, who do not know my own soul's name
have already seen her,
disguised as the shadow of a river,
saying to me:

"Cry as much as you can
for you cannot live another day without meeting God.
Your heart cannot be broken more."

When I came back into the world
all those of the world made me forget you,
saying that I'd loved you more
than anyone could love God;
God would punish me, they all said,
by making me love even more.
How can I pretend not to know you
when I have loved you since
before the day I was born?
You are among a new people,
And my soul has come here
to help me find you.

"Give up the last thing you could own,"
        she says,
"Take the last bite of food out of
        your mouth.
Give up this life."

JENNIFER DOANE UPTON

CRI

Beloved,
I have broken my wing,
beating it against the cage.
I caught sight of You,
radiant beyond bearing
and, mad with desire,
dashed against the bars.

Beloved,
I have broken my voice
on the crystal of Your true name,
trying in vain to utter
the unutterable Light.

GABRIEL BRADFORD MILLAR

STUDIO PER LA MADDALENA

by Andrea del Sarto

Before she came there were only all the men —
the fisherman, the zealot and the rest....
she was the magnetic pole, the power
of the solar plexus and the heart,
a formidable thing.

Philip's gospel says that Peter was alarmed,
the patriarch, the rock —
Christ was his province,
as Palestine was Rome's.

But Christ was her cosmos;
He blazed in her blood.
Her extravagant love, her chutzpah
lasted longer than His life.

She went to France with it
and took it underground, and knew
what even she could scarcely know.
She came up at dawn to gather berries.
No one knew when she lay down and died.

Alert below the seasons
in their loyal run,
she was vigilant as a sycamore
at the pouring spring.

The Light was in her as
a child lodges in the womb.

She delivered it slowly to the earth.

Once you have been there
do you ever really come back?

Some things are more important than your life.

GABRIEL BRADFORD MILLAR

WHAT THE I SAYS

I have come again through fire.
Through the imperative of levity
I have been in intimate
and majestic realms.

And now, through the thrust of mercy,
another chance,
and the gallant hand of gravity,
I am back.

I remember Egypt
and the inside columns,
and Greece where the temple
was the body of the god.

I am the bull,
the lion,
the eagle
and the man.

Hear this:
there is nothing
I do not survive.

There is nothing
I do not survive.

GABRIEL BRADFORD MILLAR

THE STONE SAYS

In Kabul, I didn't want to hurt the girl —
I was helpless in the hard man's hand.

I am the hidden backrest of the earth;
I will support her till I smelt in the sun.

Build your holy circle
and your house with me —

Brendan built a jolly one in Dingle
with stones like elephant feet.

But don't throw me at anyone,
please —

I was never meant
to take the place of your heart.

GABRIEL BRADFORD MILLAR

THE EARTH SPEAKS IN TUNIS

"I love you so much," she said,
"I will use every element to tell you."

So the gold wind of the sirocco
swirls in the street,
into nostrils and doorways.

The wild hair of the wind
wraps around lamps and palm trees,
twining with the night-black hair
of the women.

North, by the sea, Sidi Bou Said,
proud of its palace,
dreams of the fez.

And Carthage, its cousin,
keeps watch in the graveyard.
In its lap sleep Phoenicians and Greeks.

A young woman from England lies
roasting on the ruins
with a fever of 107,
delirious
in armoured company
and a babble of old tongues.

"South of Tunis, in the desert,
the library of stones holds
the memory of aeons,

catalogues of ravages,
floods of love surging
from the souls of saints —
the stately parade of epochs
peoples your sleep.

I am awake while
you sleep, my children;
you sleep through your life
while I work.

In a dumb dense sleep
you are merciless
to your brothers.....
that breaks my heart.

The number of times
my heart breaks
must baffle the abacus."

GABRIEL BRADFORD MILLAR

BE HORN

Be horn of plenty, heart,
be skyey, never counting costs.
Be prodigal as rain, and brave.

For the law is this:
the more love let out of the horn
the more tumbles out behind.

Though we lose the way
and dark clasps us –

how warm the breath still,
how the pain shines.

GABRIEL BRADFORD MILLAR

PAUL MATTHEWS

THE LIVING ROOM

The picture under which my father died
hangs over my fireplace now.

I always wanted it. This eagle on a pine bough
gazing upwards into the round ripe sun.

Always I assumed it was an evening coming on.
But now as I sit here in my own house

I think by his dying he has stitched a subtlety
between the eagle's eye and this red world that's rising,

and I am back with him two summers,
moving his deathbed into the living room.

That is what he wanted — to see how roses
burn in a window within the last word of a looking.

I was reading the resurrection to him when he stared
wildly into the sunlight and was gone.

GOLDEN GATE

for Gale Cook

First we heard the blue tit fluttering
in the ashes of our English woodstove.

Then the message came from California
that you had died while we slept.

No need for us to make up stories:
Our stove where the bird was trapped

burns under Hagerup's painting of the
golden gateway that you loved so much.

We only had to ease the grate
to free your happiness into our daylight.

Once upon a time you drove me sun
going down through the wine country

then suddenly asked me about the Infinite.
Surely the birds can answer it, or how

could they bring news of you five
thousand miles into such a narrow space?

PAUL MATTHEWS

RAIN AT MIDNIGHT

Alright, I can hear you. What is it
you have come to tell me, Rain?

All the people I love are not here,
but maybe you have come in answer
   to my longing for them.

I suppose you have come to tell me
there's no end to longing, and I say
what about death — isn't that
   the end of it?

There never was a time, Rain, when I
did not love you. You are oil and balm.
So, tell me what it's for — this no end
   of longing.

What if I stopped thinking there could
be an end to it and simply lived it?

I could die, I think, out beyond longing,
into the small sounds of you on the roof
   and be only the listening.

PAUL MATTHEWS

IN THE GRASS THIS MORNING

Beloved, the alphabet
glistens clean and new
in the fields this morning.

The grass on which we walk
is wet another lifetime.

*

Beloved, you must own the footprints
though the shoes be borrowed

I think the earth
which clings to them now
is not easily shaken.

*

Beloved, your lips moisten
as if an aire of summer
said you
could be its winter instrument.

*

Beloved, the gates and stiles
open a field where your beauty
always awaited me.

This crown upon my head –
I found it in the grass this morning.

PAUL MATTHEWS

THE KINGDOM THAT I LEFT BEHIND

There was a river with swans.
That's all. Now that they've flown
I can reflect upon a white reflection.

On a pure whiteness I can reflect;
Or, in a moment when I least expect,
They'll glide into the mind serene and perfect.

And indeed forever they glide in the mind
Perfect and unkind
Back there in the kingdom that I left behind.

In the kingdom of my childhood
The river in flood
Carried a fierce perfection I never understood.

I never could understand the savage grace
Of swans reflecting on the water's face.

PAUL MATTHEWS

SEBASTIAN BARKER

from BEFORE THE TIME OF THE SUNDIAL

5

Joy of my days, delight of my nights, hard partner
Walking the long paving-stones of Chelsea Embankment,
The sparkling light dandles on the grey river
The first principle of our love's bedazzlement.

You are no lady pricing the golden air,
Nor priceless statue turning in a glass museum,
For we've become one light, this light we share
Dancing the global stone through hand-held heaven.

Conspiracy of spring, behold in her
The green and lush amazement of yourself,
For you are what she is, this bed unfolding

Out of the black catastrophe of nightmare.
Redressed in clothes she hands me, I am the wealth
The rich aspire to in their tallest building.

VISITATION IN THE MOUNTAINS

How will I forget
    Sitting there, unable to write,
The white page as blank
    As my mind concentrating
On nothing so successfully
    Nothing was written?

Painfully I coaxed
    Words from the music
I heard, out of reach,
    In the fluting of the mountain streams.
Yet every word was dead
    Because of my impatience.

To write, I learn, is to be wordless.
    The words arrive in their own way,
Like a party of unexpected friends
    In evening gowns and jokey tuxedoes
Sweeping up the hidden mountain track
    Giddy with wine and laughter.

SEBASTIAN BARKER

HOLY THE HEART ON WHICH WE HANG OUR HOPE

Holy the heart on which we hang our hope.
To trust in Christ is to trust him in the torture.
Shall we believe in pastor, priest, or pope?

The love of God is learning how to cope.
I don't believe in the God you don't believe in either.
Holy the heart on which we hang our hope.

Love is a ditch in which the shallow drown.
To trust in Christ is to trust him in the torture.
Sweet is the carriage in which we come to town.

The mind like a drunkard staggers on alone.
I don't believe in the God you don't believe in either.
The sink of Sheol opens in the bone.

Love is a ditch in which the shallow drown.
The love of God is learning how to cope.
Sweet is the carriage in which we come to town.
Holy the heart on which we hang our hope.

SEBASTIAN BARKER

THE LAND OF GOLD RETURNS

The Land of Gold returns. I see
    it flashing in my brain.
The yellow leaves on dainty trees
    before my eyes again.

This is the land which God foretold
    the just and the good.
It is the land called paradise,
    the soul, the sacred wood.

I enter with my eyes lit up
    by a paradise so fair
I am alive to every scent
    in the embracing air.

I thank my God that I was born
    to walk in paradise.
It is the country of the mind
    no poet ever lost.

For poetry is what it is,
    this paradise on earth,
The Land of Gold, in which our lives
    become what they are worth.

SEBASTIAN BARKER

MORNING ROSE

I went into
a rose garden
at dawn.

The sun had just risen.
Horizontal rays
sent pink shadows.

A light wind passed.
The flowers trembled.
I looked to see

How this wind arose.
I saw it came
from the passing of God.

She was walking
in her garden
as the sun came up

Admiring her beautiful
feet which were naked.
As she passed

Air vibrated,
dew shimmered
like diamonds.

I understood

her feet represented
this dream-life.

The dew on the roses meant
the joy of manifestation
in the worlds.

And I was the witness.

As the wind covered
the feet of God
with rose-petals,

I was the witness.

AIDAN ANDREW DUN

THE TRADE

They seem erotic at remote points of cities,
eyelined in bitumen, darkest eyeshadow.
They are fine figures from a distance,
till they are seen with torn faces nearer.

They are magnificent animals of lewdness
roaming obscure backtowns and ghettos.
They are leather aphrodisiac impressions
strutting anaemic streetlight of corners.

Then you see potholes, eye-sockets
leaking black discharge of sadness,
deeply marking a deathshead with trackways
from eyes that hardly exist. The trade!

O! They are excellent silhouettes, the head
perhaps with sky-pointing blonde fountains
offering demented customers a handhold,
someone avenging a broken marriage tonight.

O! They are powerful predators of sensuality,
role-reversing omnivores, manhunters.
Then you see mainline tracks all red
along the inside arm. O my daughters!

They are fine figures from a distance
where the first glance tells a lie.
Then you see the poor face closer,
broken whore on a black raining night.

AIDAN ANDREW DUN

FIERCE MOON

Once, not long ago, yesterday even,
you loomed and dazzled, fantastic lodestar.
Just over the north horizon, just gone,
you are still an awesome curved presence.

I look at each day in a scientific light, compare
through the powerful dust-covered lens of memory.
As though all experience belonged in the past
I live in the terrible museum of our friendship.

Even now, mounting watchtowers and platforms
to stand in the observatory of real life once more,
I remember enormous trajectories, derangements
catastrophic love imposed on so-called freedom.

Planets have been destroyed, whole oceans
burnt off, evaporated in less than half a second.
I was lucky to survive your beautiful proximity.
I trust I shall never see you again, fierce moon.

AIDAN ANDREW DUN

A LINGERIE OF FLOWERS

Starry chains of daffodil suns,
skipping-ropes from the zodiac,
fall down her back.

Dangling like full moons
white peonies' perfect spheres
adorn her ears.

Ultraviolet mirror-medallions,
flowers tinted amethyst,
sway from her wrist.

Rose petals mixed with kisses,
a red ocean bitter-sweet,
regale her feet.

Snaking blue on her temples,
a crown of delphinium:
her kingdom come.

Illuminating the way to heaven,
sprays of iris, sheathes of eyes,
light up her thighs.

Diamonds at each nipple
snowdrop on her breast
when she's undressed.

Lilies in a snow-white belt
circle in a soft vortex

her milky sex.

Stars of the night-jasmine
brighten an electric air,
her atmosphere.

Bliss in the spirit comes
when the vision of her flies
through other skies.

A lingerie of flowers veils
the one called Feerique,
the one I seek.

AIDAN ANDREW DUN

MILTON'S WELL

Predestination stopped her on the road,
speeding in some overcommitment,
racing impetuous down green skylines,
pushing the envelope of the just-possible.
On an S bend with reversed camber,
on a suspicious twist of black ribbon,
fate overturned her world at sixty-five,
crushed a tin bubble with fluffy toys.
And she crawled out of a smoking hell
to stand on skid-marked tarmac, broken.

Just out of sight, hearing the sirens,
lamentations of the ambulance,
he, heretic, regicide and divorcee,
sits by the water, blind and reflecting,
rebel angel after the Restoration. Now
God sprawls on his Cavalier throne again,
after the civil war in the earthly paradise,
when sweet Oxfordshire was Lucifer's
hiding-place along the burning lake,
when tyranny was taking back the sky.

The warts on the round face of Satan,
the bogus sainthood of the King,
the cannonades of both sides, bring
sickness to the soul. His lips move.
Eve, still clutching the keys of ignition,
writes in copperplate as his whisper
interrupts the dictation of the river,

liquid sound that goes on forever,
poetry of water running over stones.

AIDAN ANDREW DUN

FIGHTING DAYS

The sun shines down
on a white table-cloth
of outspread clouds,
and we below, hungry,
quarrel over the golden specks,
occasional rays of light
that fall to the ground.

AIDAN ANDREW DUN

THE VIRGIN OF POTOSI

High in the Bolivian Tin Belt, looming over the city of Potosi, is
Cerro Rico—Rich Hill—the world's largest silver deposit, mined
since the 16th century. Here, the frustrated myth of El Dorado
coupled with industrial-scale greed created possibly the greatest
genocide in historical record. Some estimate the death-toll of Rich
Hill as high as nine million, the victims of this colonial holocaust
being chiefly Indian and African slaves. Among the exploited bizarre
quasi-Catholic animist-infused belief-systems evolved as wealth-lust
and death-cult converged.

In the white cathedrals
of the old city
there is the woman
of the graven face.

Her life-expectancy
is only thirty-five.
But she is grandmother
to her contemporaries.

Her skirt is a worm-eaten
silver-mountain
beneath which men
worship Satan with dynamite.

She has rolled away
the stone so many times
her bones stick out
through her thin brown hands.

Her tears leak down from

the shaft-top constantly.
each drop is almost
ninety-percent proof.

The son she has borne
is humpbacked, broken.
his eyes are bandaged
after three months in hell.

She has very often
seen his betrayal.
Forty silver dollars
have sold him repeatedly.

But still she gives birth
in a hand-miner's cabin;
llamas and guinea-pigs
see these nativities.

How will she find a way
through the diggings,
Americanos
conquistadors?

Her only help is
a lamp-strap tightened
to hold a single eye
firmly in place.

AIDAN ANDREW DUN

HARVEY & RAMSAY

POEM FOR OUR TIME

1894–Government agents started to divide the Hopi, People of Peace, into two opposed factions, and reported: *"In the pueblo of Oraibi, there are two factions called by the Whites the "Friendlies," and the "Hostiles." The Friendlies sent their children to school and are willing to adopt civilized ways; the Hostiles, under the bad influence of shamans, believe that the abandonment of old ways will be followed by drought and famine."* So said Sun Bôw True Brother. Hopi Katsi et Tuwa Eyesni... May the Way of Peace Prevail on Earth.

Enlightenment is simple.
Enlightenment is a Rubik's Cube.
Enlightenment is not what you think.
Enlightenment is a word.
Enlightenment is intimacy with all things.

Some things devastate
in the night-time;
where dark dreams drop us down to our knees and pray.

Two a.m. moonbeams
draw in distant American warplanes.
Nightmare treachery tracks
enemies of the state
of extraordinary rendition.
So we can Drone and Gitmo forgotten dreamers.

We, who float far from our original

homeland security
siren as Twin Towers
fall down truth
into conniving, twisted lies
in steel girders
shipped quickly
to China.

You without heartbeat,
you know what you did.
And you know what you want.
You kill freedom.
You kill wilderness.
Your skull drips black oily blood,
and your body moves
to a false tune.
You are doctor death in a mask
of tight trickery
and war crimes not addressed.

The night of darkness,
the night of no stars,
the night of no returning moon
in the desert of our wanting.
Iraq laid to waste.
Inside and outside
there is no form, feeling, cognition,
no eyes, ears, nose, body, or mind.
no mind
no mind
no mind

*Thus, I heard. On one occasion, the Blessed One was living at Gaya,
together with a thousand Bhikkhus and Bhikkhunis. "Bhikkhus and*

Bhikkhunis, all is burning. Burning with the fire of lust, with the fire of hate, with the fire of delusion. I say it is burning with birth, aging, and death. Burning with sorrow, lamentation, pain, grief, and despair. So said the Buddha.

Just know the feeling in the feeling.
Is it pleasant, unpleasant, or neutral?
Bud-dho, attend within each heartbeat.
Bud...with the in breath.
Dho...with the out breath
Direct mindful awareness to feeling
Pleasant, unpleasant, or neutral...?

It is unpleasant.
Consuming fire of outrage
shoots searing sensations
into our flesh core
Frozen grief at deceitful ruin
aches every living cell.
Weighted stones
of dreaded despair
pull the heart down
through each vertebra
into softening tissue
and oxygenated blood
pumping pain.

Chemical dissonance
surges into brain coordination
and scrambles sanity.
Trauma releases into the world.

The beast has no holding.
It roams and scavenges

the desecrated, rotting flesh
of grandiose structures
that peel away from
our faded, fast, Capitalist Gods
who abandon us all
in the end.

Here, enlightenment lands
like a sick thump to the stomach.

At night we track mala beads
along the wild stations of our heart
so we can know
the lost islands of our soul,
like animals at a dry water hole.

*Earth is rapidly headed towards a catastrophic breakdown if humans
don't get their act together. The world is headed towards a tipping point
marked by extinctions and unpredictable changes. The Earth is going to be
a very different place. We are to be pushed through the eye of the needle of
political strife, economic strife, war, and famine.* So say the scientists.

This being human is a guest house
of toxic dumped wastelands.
Every morning a new arrival
where life grows no more.
Meet them at the door laughing
at our insane leap to death.
Or screaming
through the abandoned stations of heart.
Or collapsed on the sofa
shooting up the drug of our choice
so we can forget
and not feel

our dissolving into oblivion. This
is...is not,
is not human.
We are not humane any more.

We, the machine,
testify against ourselves
as our future screams towards us.
Machiavellian corporate psychopaths
swarm through every cell
like millions of dead bees
of media words
spewing onto streets of choking cities.
Our floating dear heart
knots and twists
downwards
pulled by the gravitational
collapsing empire
of the wall's inevitable seduction
into total destruction.

Stranded people struggle
to pull the needle out
from raised veins
of unhappiness
as they fall
under the belly
of the crazed
fossil fuel dinosaur

Earth haunts another waking night
weeping her beloved species
disappearing.

Terror from the slaughterhouse
reaps horrific carnage
of concentration camp
vicious violence
feeding sadomasochistic depravity
of no human, anymore.
Animals as objects twisted
into iron bar cages of no mercy.
Artificially inseminated, castrated,
ejaculated, plucked, crushed, torn, trashed,
boiled, and skinned alive.

Our human heart flees
the intimacy of all things
as a terror tsunami of black karma arrives.

Good-bye tigers;
Good-bye lions;
Good-bye elephants;
Good-bye rhinos;
Good-bye orangutan;
Good-bye humble bumblebee;
Good-bye coral reefs;
Good-bye albatross;
Good-bye Amazon River;
Good-bye Arctic Circle;
Good-bye us all...

Hello raging, elemental storms of the world's end.

Nirvana: *cessation of burning, the taintless, the truth, the other shore, the subtle, the everlasting, the invisible, the undifferentiated, the deathless, peace, the blest, safety; exhaustion of craving, the wonderful, the*

marvellous, non-hostility, freedom, the island, the shelter, the harbour, the
refuge, the beyond, the end. So said the Buddha.

So pause at the gate of no returning
at the edge
of the hedge
end game.

Here *Shariputra*, balances perilous survival
twisting in the wind of our whims.
Here *Shariputra*, the brave leap of reclamation.
Our deepest heart implores it,
with liquid, fluid prayer.
So turn the mad mind around
from its callous scalpel to the world.

From the collapsing furnace of known lands
fierce and urgent cries mop up denial.
Millions sign: All Out Now!
Quick, before it's too late
to walk again
in the rose-scented garden
where your soul patiently waits
among shattered fragments
of the empire
to break down your wall
of small expectations
and from nightmares
pull you awake.

Here is the faith of wild warriors
Who leave dream-thinking far behind.
Who leap beyond the walls of the mind.
Who know the intimacy of all things.

And who return to this, our human
that feels the scream
in each mindful moment
and chooses
to soften.
To breathe the mystery.
To enter the unknown gate.
To love fiercely every living thing,
right down to the last blade of grass.

Quick, time, any time.
Here and now will do.
Move beyond your walled pastimes
to join the Awakening.
Time yourself out
from the needle of craving
and boogie down with intense
flamenco, disciplined passion
so we can crash the machine.

Soar over the edge
on the breath of our heart's sorrow
and make a beloved circle
outside the wall
where the storehouse of untamed dreams
will decolonize our mind.

On the dark horse
of their unfolding,
the warriors march in tune
to her victorious soft truth
unwrapping hearts
that shatter

tight psychopathic masks
and the intensity of our madness
as we upturn
the cavern of denial
and the collapsing cave
of our ancestral wounds,
over which we leap.

We might pray, wail,
and sometimes fail.
But here we fall at the feet
of that with no name,
which has all names printed
into our authentic heart
woven into each part
of joyous, sane, and connected
primordial ease.
Do it now— if not now...when?

Death of the planet won't wait for another time. The "perhaps"
and the "maybe."

*Those who set forth on this path should give birth to this thought:
"Whatever living beings there are, in whatever realms, I shall work to free
them. And though I free living beings, not a single being is liberated. And
why not? No one can be a bodhisattva who creates the perception of 'a self,'
of 'a being,' of 'a life span,' or of 'a soul.'"* So teaches the Diamond
Sutra.

Still, if someone should lean towards you
on a cold, forsaken night
inviting you to leave your castle wall,
lean with her into your deepest hope.
Because the storm is coming

Do you feel the ardent scream
in our heart molten agony
rising on fire
from the torture of the Earth?

I dream a wild forest
of parrots and monkeys.
Maybe one day,
We will return.

Earth dust walkers
together
through the tangle,
we stumble
to return
wild shamanic power
of the hearts
pure peace pulse.

In quiet release of identification,
from the fired and wired
off-sync brain
merged with the machine,
prajna intuitive intelligence
of the deep
rewires.
She
pours living truth into us
and leads our way home.

• True Heart home;

- Soft Heart home;
- Fierce Heart home;
- Generous Heart home;
- Merciful Heart home;
- Swift Protection Heart;
- Invincible Courage Heart;
- True Refuge Heart;
- Destroyer of Negativity Heart;
- Bliss and Equanimity Heart;
- Remover of Sorrow Heart;
- Transformer of Poison Heart;
- Serene Peace Heart;
- Distribution of Wealth Heart;
- Impeccable Virtue Heart;
- Joy and Laughter Heart;
- Sublime Intelligence Heart;
- Creative Wisdom Heart;
- Worthy of Honour Heart;
- Foundation in Freedom Heart;
- Radiant Health Heart;
- Ferocious Compassion Heart;
- All Victorious Heart;
- Complete Enlightenment Heart;
- Aware Heart;
- Present Heart;
- Avalokitesvara, Hands and Eyes Heart.

Gate Gate Paragate

This mantra is true and not false.
Mother of the Buddhas.
Matrix of creation.

Empty of all distinctions.
Your true heart hears all beings,
their beginning and their end.
Your true heart is not the seer or seen,
and it is both.
Just this!
Parasamgate Bodhi Svaha.

Everything now means nothing,
except how much
you reclaim your human
that loves your life
your Earth
your all other living beings
and every flower pushing through concrete
on your way to work.

Because this is the moment you've waited for.
The moment for wild prayer,
flash mobs,
and for occupying the corners of fascist madness.
Sit your ground.
Stake your truth.
And should you be brave,
then shout out
to the far corners of the walls
until the force of our sound together
demolishes every carefully positioned brick.

*I feel that tonight I shall die, for I am wounded by an arrow, and the
wound is telling me that I shall die. The bite of the wound is fierce, and the
mouth of the wound does not heal, but it swells and throbs so that my flesh
aches and I burn with pain and feel my heart falling. I know I shall not see
the break of another day, for my heart feels I am to die, and I cannot bear*

to think of the smell of springbok. But as for you, you must look after the children, you must keep them with you, you must keep them beside you, you must not take your eye from them, you must not give them away to strangers, you must keep a good fire so that the cold does not kill them. And though I will be dead, I will think of you and the children. I speak to you, holding up your heart so that you may understand. Told by //Kabbo of the First Sitting There People.

Time with relentless harvesting
your precious human life
is short.
As all life
gathers proof of our faith
through the pilgrimage of the night
that tests the grounds of our being,
so we may know
the measure of courage
and the wellspring of our heart,
from which we sip nectar.

Just as the brown, striped bug
drinks from the white elderflower,
and the orange, thin-winged butterfly
skips through ochre grasses,
and the grey, knowing wolves
move through cold, white snow,
and the rhinos through dry, bush veldt,
go as lions stalk impala
along the river slow.

Slow is the Earth's rhythm,
deep and unfathomable in our collective soul.
The rhythm of the days tick-tock,
winding through the web of our connection

of Internet consumption
where we search what we hope to know.

Because to truly know is to not know
And to not know
is so much evidence of where faith can go.

*It is like a great regal tree growing in the rocks and sand of barren
wilderness. When the roots get water, the branches, leaves, flowers, and
fruits will all flourish. The regal tree of awakening growing in the
wilderness of birth and death is the same. All living beings are its roots; all
buddhas and bodhisattvas are its flowers and fruits. By serving all beings,
by serving this great Earth, by pouring the water of living, gentle, and
fierce compassion, together we will embody the flowers and fruits of our
true awakening. And even when the realms of empty space are exhausted,
the realms of living beings are exhausted, the karmas of living beings are
exhausted, and the afflictions of living beings are exhausted, we will still
accord with this, our deepest heart, endlessly, continuously, in thought after
thought, without cease. Our body, speech and mind never weary of this
service."* So says our true heart.

Gate Gate Paragate Parasamgate Bodhi Svaha

THANISSARA

SIMON HELPS CHRIST CARRY THE CROSS

I was looking over the wall, in the heat of the afternoon,
Listening to the silence of the burning road;
When around the corner came a crowd: of beggars,
Lepers, soldiers and pregnant women, talking low.
The dust from their sandals blotted out the sun.
Then it was that I felt thirsty,
And, seeing the fig trees full in my garden,
Reached and plucked, and bit into the flesh.

The rest came very fast. I fought, not wanting to go:
My own worries were plenty. They threw the fig fruit
Out of my hand and put there this staggering man's cross:
My fingers are stained, but with sap or blood?
Nights now are sleepless from my shoulder's pain;
No fig, no vinegar satisfies my thirst.

THE DISMEMBERED SPIRIT: XII

Hard, for a man, the telling to his mother
The death of her favourite son; how the waves break
Now in the dark hallway, over the brother
Unwanted, pitched away out of love's wake.

She grasps death like a lover in her bony arm,
For his grave-clothes she pulls down the skies.
Grief's a changeling heart that wills no balm
But strangles in its wanting other lives.

Climb to bed, daddy. Sleep. My duty now to hear
In silence on the stairway her distilled
Marital contempt, indifference, tears
For the one she loved until it killed.

Heartbreak, your court is here and you've dined well.
I'll fight all my father's life to crack your hell.

HILARY DAVIES

WALK HERE WITH ME

Walk here with me. We do not know how long.
The braided waters cross the marsh beside Bomb Crater
                                        Pond.
Bullrushes sing by the causeway,
In the leafing copses. And through the air we hear
The tumble of the swallows, their high-cloud mewing.
The sun was all around us. O my darling
How in the harvest of our days we were
And on the swans' backs the pearls of life
Streamed.

            Now the water of your breath
Breaks in a rainbow over each moment
We walked together where the willows and alders
Stretch their arms heavenward
And the cormorants circle
Over the rowers – o so full of life! –
Beating into the future.
But here, see, my heart is hung on the hawthorn
For you with your stoop stride never
Never never will walk by my side
Along the sweet Lea river nor lift your head
To hear the geese cry keening, ever again.

HILARY DAVIES

IN THE PUMPING STATION, MARKFIELD PARK

I stood in the pumping house by the great machine.
Men moved around her. Black, red, white, gold, green
She moved in her prism of steam. The rafters and children
                                           waited.
Summer light fell on the rainbowed floor.
And through the window I saw you sitting in the rose garden
Still as the flowers you watched.

                 The clouds rose higher and higher
Filling the steel vaults and the roof of heaven,
Tower upon tower and columns of hope building
Till all was white and desirous and ready.

Then the lever fell. The faintest tremble
Like a sublime monster waking from sleep
Before the oil like silk drew up the pistons from some well
Deep within. On what wheel of white and gold and green
We flowered in the pumping house as the axle span.

Even so you watched as one by one
The rose links opened and parted
And I saw you borne away on them,
Floating out from time's dynamo in the pumping station
Floating away above the roaring world
Out over the marsh and the estuary and down to the sea
On the ark everlasting.

HILARY DAVIES

IN THE RHINE WOOD

A man sang in the wood
Whose bird cries filled my days
Their sip and sweep and swallow,
Their bunter and chatter,
Their high, longing curl over the trees' tips.

A man sang in the wood
And the whole forest leant forward.
The valley floor boomed back his melody
And the walls of the combe closed round.

A man sang in the wood.
I never saw him, imagined his legs thrown forward in the
                                        sun.
So he passed along the river, and sang
As the motes and the butterflies
Rose and sank in the waterlight
And the blackbirds a thousand fold answered him.

HILARY DAVIES

HARVEY & RAMSAY

THE ICON

for Sophia

this fury and sorrow
is of the icon
emanating from the icon

who works for pharaohs
is seen in falcons
and carvings of falcons

there is no tomorrow
for man or woman
but in the woman

who in her burrow
a mind is making
an intelligence is making

as bow-and-arrow
its target is seeking
its tip is seeking

to pierce the marrow
of the living token
and the dying token

the falcon is furrowed
its god is forsaken

its cosmology is forsaken

for ones and zeros
the images are broken
the icon is broken

NIALL MCDEVITT

TO A LION-SKIN RUG

for Palash

Does a lion think? Not of ending its days in a stately home
as a trophy at the top of the staircase, two-dimensional,
the bulk scavenged off to a light-brown, flat, floppy pancake
draped in an archway, a nothing in lion's clothing;
no leonine tools of the trade, no Coeur de Lion pumping
the blood of a Richard to flex his claws on Saracen sands,
dead to the world, a mini-desert with a hairy dune:
the deathshead (twisted up to seem it's still roaring but

looking like it suffers from a neck disorder called torticollis);
really just a pussycat, safe for an Aesopian mouse
to play in the jaws or tiptoe along the whiskers,
debate with dull orange eyes from a position of strength
and out-squeal the über-miaow, out-scuttle the loping stride
of the golden killer who can't even manage a bowl
of Kit-e-Kat. Is it thinking now? Not of chicken liver chunkies
but dreaming of Sekhmet, her womanly hips and breasts, her cobra.

NIALL MCDEVITT

(Note: Sekhmet is the Egyptian goddess of war, woman with
lion's head, star of the Egyptian Room at the British Museum).

THE LABOUR MART

(after reading 'Morning Dissertation' by David Gascoyne)

in rooms you sadden, or stretch, in the rooms of our solitude
and touched, maybe, with a butterfly-coloured crisis
fountaining from the crown. a green tea assuages
the blueness of veins. there is calm to intellectually cross
bridges – engineered of finesse – to where who you are
finds itself in new companies of caring thaumaturges
tapping compositions on keys for you to learn
how keys are keys in and out of customary cells

in rooms you have no say, negatively capable,
even as you spy on a green-tabarded builder
crossing the scaffold along the opposite semi-detached house
confidently, in a white helmet, he can see you
also. his task is not literary or alchemical
but in dreams he has built an upside-down pyramid
balancing on its tip, spinning like a top
as you've laid words menially as bricks.
your consciousnesses have intermingled. he works in the sun
cutting a black bin-liner into squares for his colleague
squatting behind the chimney, drilling, fixing tiles

they move about the roof's slant with a panther's agility
in the few hours of daylight left to them, unprecious.
they won't – they can't – be there by night. even if you look
the men in their decades will disappear.

work if you can

NIALL McDEVITT

A MOTHER

what has happened to
me
that I can sit with coffee
in the smokes of the streetcars
in the smokes of Greek cigarettes
not my own
and see a mother
as if through crystal
completely made of whiteness
completely made of light
shining from glass tables
as if closer than the sun
falling
orangely from her ears and shoulders
into her own reflection
passed from one city
one country
to another
costume-changing to angel now
even amid rasping motorbikes
or under rutting helicopters
and not just anyone
but the mother I'm with?

where is this? Africa
in an egg-yolk heat?

even as she smokes
the Sophia is flowering

NIALL McDEVITT

BURN

(O' Prophet!) Say to the believing men that they cast down their looks and guard their private parts - that is purer for them; surely Allah is aware of what they do. And say to the believing women that they cast down their looks...

the burn of male eyes on streets, the burn of female eyes back, the burn of male eyes from behind a keffiyeh on Saladin Street, the burn of female eyes from behind a hijab on Herod's Ascent, the burn of male eyes in Silwan, the burn of female eyes in Sheik Jarrah, the burn of male eyes is felt, is met with the burn of female eyes, the burn is felt, the burn is met, the male eyes and female eyes, clashing comets, showering meteors, the male eyes burn for beauty and revolution, the female for virtue and equality, the male eyes burn for virtue and equality, the female for beauty and revolution, the burn of male eyes on streets, the burn of female eyes back, male and female eyes return burn for burn

cool with the coolness of the pool of Siloam

still with the stillness of the pool of Siloam

burning in Silwan, burning in Sheik Jarrah, from behind a keffiyeh, from behind a hijab

the soft jewellery of the eyes isn't durable, it burns its hour

(Jerusalem, 2014)
NIALL McDEVITT

VISITATION OF THE SWANS

This was the action of the crazy woman.
That morning when the swans came she ran
all the way to the dairy, filled the big pewter jug
the shiny two gallon one, she filled it with milk.
Then she came rushing, staggering with effort
—for she was only a spindle-shanks herself—
she came to the lake milk spilling over her cracked shoes
and the swans raised their heads interestedly, like snakes,
pure cold white snakes their necks weaved at her.
One great bird roused up and beat its powerful wings
then they began to sail towards her as she lifted the jug
and poured a huge white arc across the brackish water.
Milk splashing sheer white as snow, not cream
but salt white and the ice brightness of the swans
drifted into its curve as she stood calling out
O my White Queens, my Beauties, my lost wild songs,
O loves... So she stood, calling out their miracle,
and they dipped their red beaks, siphoned the milk
as I believe whales suck krill, or flamingoes ingest
the tiny red crustaceans that fire their feathers,
so the swans drank the whiteness off the water,
their amazing necks scooping, dipping.
She placed her jug down on the thin grass,
stretched out her hands as if the plumage
of those frosted birds could warm her, while beyond us
the people who had come to see the swans cheered
and someone sang. Others threw our black seed bread;

it is wholesome, but the swans refused it.

All that day, people came running down the broken roads,
came by horse or van just to watch the strange birds
skim and glide the water. When the milk was gone
the lake seemed calmer than before, black, quite polished
and the swans were doubled in its mirror. That night
they shone luminous as moons under the willows,
and we kept watch. At last, our children understood
the grace in the constellation of Cygnus.
The swans were with us three days.
Afterwards, the snow came again
and it grew intensely cold — cold as poverty.

ROSE FLINT

ELEMENTS OF HEALING

Here, they will place a shock of fire on your heart
so your body will remember its living rhythm again,
and how your heart can be warm, when it loves.

They will place exotic liquid chemicals
or someone else's blood in needles and syringes,
pierce your own routes of water, (those blue conduits
roaring with tides and memories, moods of the moon)
and they will sail you to safe shore.

They will catch the air for you, in tubes and soft boxes
transparent as flayed angel's skin
and they will breathe for you, slowly, seriously
kiss you back into life.

On your tongue they will place willow and rosy periwinkle
chalks and six kinds of sugar, wafered like bread,
your body will respond, flesh to flesh, turn away from hurt
to blossom and make new, delicious fruit.

They will allow the cool magic of ether to move you
from days crowded with clawed fears
into a healing night peaceful as old black winter velvet.
Then your spirit will grow strong and lovely as amaryllis
that needed a spell of cold darkness before it bloomed like a
                                                    star.

                                    ROSE FLINT

WALKING WITH SPIDERWOMAN

If I trust the web
I can walk across it, like she does, Spider
Grandmother, her feet as accurate as light.

If I trust the web
I will remember that she weaves me
and you, beloved, in your tower of noisy glass.

I will remember that she weaves me
and Time's million deaths
of tribes and wolves and cougars, wildcat
kitten skins sold for just five dollars in the store.

She weaves the dance. Death is a colour
in the rainbow, all destructions of our hearts;
I have to trust her wisdom, remember
she knows Time in its multiple dimensions.

I have to trust her wisdom, remember
without vision her fine silk line that only sometimes
catches starlight, glints against space deep
as nothingness. Trust this: step out across the dark

remembering that she weaves me
and that when I cross, I carry shining thread.

ROSE FLINT

MAY TIDE

Beltane

The may blooms late this year; leaves unfurling
their green in curving hedges, a surf of white flowers
edging rippling seas of dark grass ripening to blaze.
Hawthorn is lighting the fuse of the fire
that powers the Universe, the live wire
our sappy red hearts are strung on, beating, beating
for love of all this wet juicy salty earthy rising.

Full moon slipping up the sky: lawns glow white.
as lakes. I feel little blossoms open under my skin
like promises, little fishes, charms, fizz and electric.
If I stand still enough I can hear trees catch their breath,
river's liquid singing, I feel the world shiver
as the great enchantment of Summer
thickens around me in blue, half dark, half-starred light.

Stand naked on cold grass,
let flowers escape from your lips and fingertips,
call your lover out from the black oak shadows.
Tonight, the Goddess of Love races her white horses
in a tidal wave that floods through suburban gardens,
through sleep-shut farms and safari parks,
over sleek formal lawns and allotments;
she is breaking down walls and terraces,
transforming clipped topiary to sinuous wolves
and great cats snarling their heat, claws gleaming;
she is raising mist in the valley, steam of hot bodies

finding connection. In the hollow throat of the hill
a woman sways like a white willow wand,
arches back as her lover bends closer and deeper—
a flurry of white petals caught in her hair like pearls.

Never too late to catch the wave that turns the tide
as Beltane blossoms get under our skin and red fire
rises though blood, the great pulse drumming
the wild dance of joy that carries beauty into the future.

ROSE FLINT

SPIRIT PATHS

And what I hope for every winter is to find a way through
to the other side where the jubilant light begins again
in a hesitation of birdsong.

I am learning to see in the dark, recognise that *this is a sign*
and this, these sudden sensual chances and clues
—as in melodic fifths on the radio or a rain-diadem,
or the unexpected arrival of white cyclamen in cellophane—
things the body perceives first as elements of light
and offers up to the spirit, so shut in its hole, mole-blind.

And there are the synchronicities that puzzle you
but make me shiver with their meanings: three aligned
heron feathers or the time and thought of meteorites;
I bring them back to you like trophies from a race of joy.

I had always believed I would die young
not making the markers of thirty nor forty-five.
In a way then, this is all extra and more risky than any year,
this precious time of coming-to-knowing,
but even my acceptance of what is, is, can't fully protect me;
Autumn still brings the familiar fear: Winter will be here
and I will be in darkness, groping forward nervously
trying to remember that the black dragons
and dogs of shadowland are guided by dark mothers
carrying secret gifts of pearl —still I'll cry for kinder weather.

This then, is the origin of fear: that the sun will not rise

and there will be no release from the dark; this, set beside
our knowing of how we must wait always for the hour
when we will not go on into the next season.
Like a film of ghosts, the family, the quick rivers and flowers,
the music and horses will stream past us
covering the brightening land as we are turned aside
into a strangeness we can only trust.

This morning the air reminded me of the country
where we learned to love each other; I know now
that was not better than this. All our symbols and armoury
all our footsteps and collisions are spirit paths, showing
the way through, complex and simple as the lines
held by my hands; and how I hold love between them.

ROSE FLINT

JAY RAMSAY

from INTO THE HEART (A MATRIX POEM)

A child stands in a garden.
You cry, and then you see him.
He cries, you have forgotten him.
You cry from a well so deep
There is no end to your tears, but beginning.

He is no cipher, but the real thing;
His face is your own, the years are nothing.
She holds you, then you hold him—
You hold him, and he is golden
He transforms, he conducts your wedding.

He smiles, he teaches you with grass
In a handful sprinkled over your knees.
He has answered you: you understand him,
Not even you could fail to now—
As you say at last 'this is me, this is me'

ANGEL OF THE NORTH

for Donna Salisbury

Astonishing the air—
wings-up alert as if just landed
out of the invisible's so much greater realm

and yet rooted as only presence can be
dwarfing the small hill become its base
above bushes in their sunlit spring-yellowing blaze
set against blue sky on this postcard...

And then who are you, bird-man, with your faceless face
your wing-struts stretched as wide as a jumbo jet's—
and the androgynous line of your body
rippling into solid merged gale-withstanding feet
where the weathered steel becomes wood so nearly
                                        breathing?

In one pair of eyes, for as long as it takes
to begin to absorb the amaze of you, I want to say
you are more purely here than we may know
not only created and cast, winched and hefted, inch by inch
but as a Being in the guise of the earth
and all our folly you stand beyond, transforming it
in the standing shape of your vigil

—as the road swings, as the camera pans,
in the flight of any bird's wings, around you—

and not as crucifixion now, but witness

to the greater world you announce that never leaves us
however ridiculous we are
waiting and waiting for us to awaken
and scale the hill-mound's tiny distance to you, for always.

JAY RAMSAY

FOURTEEN LINES FOR BRITAIN

Re-imagine this island, once called great
not merely motorway-scarred, a broken mirrorscape
but as a beginning of what we must become
if we are to live as one world people—

and we are its molten confusion, fired to ash:
smutty news, broken schools, littered roads
our heads held low, our hearts afraid
under the parade of all we are supposed to want...

But raise your eyes—and your glasses, friends—
where the fantasy fails is where life can be as she is
and Albion can rise, phoenix like again,
buffed bright as a wind-filled spinnaker

our hope where we live, in every village and street
in all we can do for each other, and the God of Love.

JAY RAMSAY

ONLY LISTEN

Culbone Valley, NE Somerset
(i.m. Joan D'Arcy Cooper)

Imagine what might happen
if you shut your mouth and listened:

you might fall into a thousand
pieces of light

each irradiated
with birdsong and blue sky

each of them speaking
your original name.

In all your senses —
hearing, tasting,
touching, smelling, and sensing
fill them with listening

and you will find yourself again.

                    *

And when you have become your listening
your breath will heal you of all misgiving

and all the tightness you have held
all over your body and being

will become a babbling stream of healing,
caressing and soothing, sustaining every cell...

and you will be the one you always were within,
who silently lives underneath everything.

    *

And if you listen, high above the sound of the water
in the sun-dappled beech trees like a church built
all around the birdsong—you may hear

a flute: dipping, and gliding, and soaring
in and out of the stillness of a dream...

And long after the girl who played the flute has gone
you will hear, or imagine you hear, her song...

half-heard between the leaf-breeze and the stream
where it has become your listening.

JAY RAMSAY

from SUMMERLAND

METANOIA
Gk. 'to turn around, to be changed'

17.

What is the turning ?
First we must see
a world that's unreal
we're sure is reality.

Snow thickly falling
shrouding us in cloud.
We've lost our bigger story
linking us to Source.

Instead we have...Santa Claus ?
Our so-called big society,
its vain political promises
and substitute sky.

One global village, maybe
but abstracted above the land
our own true feelings
replaced by instant chat.

This is the realm of Ahriman
bonding us to matter
that we think we 'must have'
filling the inner void

while Lucifer gazes on
a lopsided Narcissus
full of his own image
only Christ, the 'I', can counter

standing between them...
and without our being there
we're living in a driven dream
where Money is God

worship and security
until the bubble bursts
the rug is pulled —
it all falls through

till we start to see
we must have sufficiency
not greed, our wants and needs
hopelessly confused, fused

growth at any price —
resources privatized —
and money, our social currency
that only exists because we trust it

toyed with like a sex shop doll
by the private sector, for itself
only returned through us
to the realm of common good.

Meanwhile the world is on fire
and we are on fire with it
feeling it as we never have

intolerable as it is

(there's nowhere to turn
a blind eye to anymore...

issues come out
of every crack and door—)

all in one crucible, flask, athanor
the gold of a thousand mornings
hidden in the blackening
and this saltwash of tears.

Earth, our circumference
and wholeness in Creation
we have to return to,
the wisdom of ages

the living Book of Nature
burnt to our reading
until we break free
of our techno-idolatry

coming back to soul, source
the Living Word, love
breathing here among us
within all our names for it

beyond all our conditions
freed from manipulation
become the thing itself
in manifestation...

Love, our salvation
one church across the world
one faith, one turning
in the ground of our being

Love in this turning
of everything between us
from hate into seeing
all we have been

and these fragile flames of hope
tealights lit in a line
quivering in the morning sun,
back in the Garden of Life

the evening lights of the town
glittering, bejewelled, neon
in the whitening dark
that is Bethlehem and birth.

This is our story
where we all have a place
in how we live and choose
and move through every day

beyond you, me and she — we
unfolding this tapestry
that is all we can be
in truth and beauty.

One World People
among the diamond seeds of dawn.

JAY RAMSAY

BLESSED UNREST

'Follow your bliss? Follow your heartbreak'
— Andrew Harvey

The geese are gathering above the Findhorn shoreline
their wild entwined cries, a cacophony of threads
late at night and in the dark before the dawn;
harbingers. And to the shots that greet them
from the underlings of the death machine —
casual or culling, you hardly care
but it sharpens their cries like a pencil
twisted round in the socket of its blade
in your heart: and you want to go out
armed with nothing but your outrage
and always now, with their cries echoing
in all your blessed unrest.

Blessed ? Yes, their unsleep
your reason for living
this world's passionate awakening
to sense beyond sense
and the litanies of its non-sense,
the same fire that you follow
into the depth of your heartbreak
that brings up the sun
in the heart of a lion
speaking the Holy Name.

JAY RAMSAY

SHARD

for the women...Saving the Arctic

The very thought of it
could make your palms sweat.

Sheer dizzying ascent of glittering hot glass ice !

Scaling it, this monument
spire of spires
bared under a Godless sky
pyramid of Mammon
where only corporations rule...Pharoahic
summit sheared off like a knife
tip snapped to skeletal scaffolding...

And six women with rucksacks, in helmets
six spunky angels faithful to a higher cause
than passive acceptance, tailing each other
feeding back thin white rope
to just over a thousand feet—

Passing a gobsmacked windowcleaner
and a black waitress at the 30th floor
poised with her tray in her hand, as if frozen

Not even the police dare intervene
they're way beyond —
only monitored by their transport counterpart
via telescope, perhaps ?
As they inch towards the stars

To unfurl the highest banner in the world
to shame Shell free of its rationalizations,
its lying polite business-speak
its pretend-God-horizon
where all is harmless and under control
(as it is secretly planned)
cold as the Arctic itself
whitewashed and snowblind
so all they can do is climb, and keep climbing
(no way back down)

the impossible mountain of the untransformed world
on the edge of our fragmented time

towering over all three offices far below
and the trains, you tweet, 'like electric worms'
and the millions of us in London's bloodstream
and every where this image is seen in
that want a future we can believe in
but have less and less idea where to look
(other than at each other—)
without closing our eyes

could raise them now
to what we can be
when we reach again for the sky.

11 July 2013, London

JAY RAMSAY

ST. IVES

The swing and swish of the waves breaking in,
the sea like the planet breathing in our sleep

each suck, hiss, and pause of drawing back...

as I breathe, or don't breathe, and want to be as it
as deeply with you in my arms, in your arms
Mother of the Sea.

Mother who gave us breath, breathe me.

All saints, and the souls of the dead
who know that life eternal is inside the breath
say listen to the sea, and surrender to the sense

that takes you beyond form and name and memory,
fathered in your birth and death
by the Father of the Air

and the whisper in my ear on this driftwood bench...
the car that purred past on this sidestreet like a silhouette
in the still dawn pre-dawn, lingering...

like the warmth between us as I finally come back to bed.

Wherever you are, come back to your breath.

JAY RAMSAY

ALWAYS

Sometimes the night brings him in
in the fold of a fox's bark
or the eager wailing of cats.
And you are sitting by the fireside
where the coals pursue their private Etna,
country of molten caverns,
the lava dragons shifting in their lair.
The pages of your book lie open,
the thronged words running on without you
—lives to be lived and fought out by chapter—
independent of attention.
You have your own stories dreaming themselves
in the rich tresses of memory,
all the tones of hope, anxiety, laughter, discontents,
the palpable skein of what love is.

You turn to meet its glance.

And night has brought him in.
The chair is empty,
the quiet hearth settled.
Yet just beyond sight
he stands in the silence where touch was,
enfolds you in the wings of rest.
Later will come the sharp tang of dawn;
stars fall to brighten grass,
the chattering pigeons, the early-rising pheasant.
Still lingers the embrace,
unspoken now, transcendent.

ABOVE LAMORNA COVE

And a great sound that might have been Rilke's song
rose up over the mud-stubbled field
as though the sussuration of the seas
poached the land for a sigh's length,
brought its waters over the cliff
reminding us of when they covered the earth and will do again,
soon now, soon now

and the breath flocked up in wings
for it was birds after all, fieldfare
lifting from the soil in a dark arc of feather
that seemed one only, all quills bent
to the thermal in an instinct of journey,
the sure imperative of the avian;
as though the once-ordered seasons will be infinite.

ZANNA BESWICK

DIMENSION

    Voice said 'angel' and
I heard the word as one might
    see a poker card

    spiral onto the
pillow: ace of diamonds.
    'Reflection' whispers

    the angel and down
white corridors of time dis-
    appears without me

ZANNA BESWICK

IN THE NAME

Let me fly down the path of the eagle
        steep mountainside
tumble on air
through forest tops glide

Let the sun catch my wing
as eucalyptus branches
reach for silver
        their sloughed bark
        trailing in my wake

Let the small marsupial
crouch under tree fern
hearing the crack of my feathers
the taut skin drumming
        along the creek

Let the moon rise on the falls
as I skim down the spray
        vertiginous and glorious

Let the sweep of eagle's eye
be scope of my vision.

ZANNA BESWICK

WATTAMOLLA ROCKS, NEW SOUTH WALES

She speaks in the rock
this lady of the lagoon;
her skin is the sealskin
in eucalyptus shade
where lizards like fishes
escalate through sand.

Her voice visits cormorants
she whispers in flecks of spray
splashing in her mirrors,
not cowed by the distant thunder
of travellers; spreads sandstone skirts
squatting between splayed roots.

Around her, afternoon settles.
What she speaks
is in the ear of the wind,
the throat of winged honeyeater.
I catch not a syllable
but what heart sings

and hand lets go –
as a butterfly on opened palm
pauses
lays its dappled colour suddenly
to the breeze
and is free.

ZANNA BESWICK

PETER OWEN JONES

IMOGEN

In these fathoms
lie wind and rain kept still, until
a swinging moon ferments a loosening
of knots; of measure's ropes
and hardened oaths
tattered on fences of sky and skin
only half-hearing the sins of thieves
opening the door to the storm —

So she wraps the birds
in hedges, strips the fish
to the depth, she swears
to hold the meadow, the yard, the churn
to know the swelling of her waves

and the drowning of men.

THE PARK

Estranged from rain and rattling air
this house is falling. Inside we inject
treasons conversing now with the
few that remain, some dead glass eyes
and fading feathers.

The jingle birds sing drowning what is
lost and what is teetering. We are stooped
with soap-washed hands scrubbing fields
and forest floors as the trees turn ill.

It is just reason raiding the bower,
yes: flatten the waves
scour the gorse, new roses
do nothing but weep…
May sings a snow as the captain's
course remains unchanged.

The witnesses deaf
to crying leaves
the corpses of trees
the bees are prophesying and
the finches singing psalms.

PETER OWEN JONES

THE STILL

Rain and sun from one
sky feed the searching sea
that does not need our knowing.
Only a fool measures the wind.

There is nothing to be gained from
counting grains of dust, numbering hairs;
you cannot feel the churn
of rooks swinging the skies
in the tins of your years.

Bring the stags into the cities !
To think we have covered
rivers in stones
turned fish blind, heated the seas
and still the incense swings;
still we believe.

Come, come sit with Shanti
hear the bridges fall —
take the cactus needle until leaves speak,
nasturtiums burn,
until you have cried enough tears
to wash in.

Share the bread with the birds,
the wine with the rivers,
and they will tell you *every breath
is song.*

PETER OWEN JONES

CLUSTERS

One song sings the wave to the shore
and the flies cascade in an alley
lined with light, taking the mercy
of rain and air.

Watch the waters'
swelling cells
still and sometimes screaming,
leaning on our death.
Old men do not swim.

Inland, the air swills spring.
Afraid at first, hardly daring to live
the leaves creep into the wind
and the fields are white with rain.

Reason is no cure for madness.
In which book do we write the blossom,
that in time Tryfan's stubborn stones
will melt
as the prophecies of physics burn,
the stems and bitter flies
the dancing oaks and shapes of shells
return the earth to fluid red
regressing to its birth ?

The temple is made of leaves;
do not bind it with stories.

PETER OWEN JONES

THE SEVENTH

Driving past Littlington,
the Wilmington road
the river's grove on the left,
a meadow of easy cows
the towers of Alfriston above,
the channels dug in fields.

There's a plank across the water
the colour of beer —
small purple sloes hidden
in burnt leaves, and all these ducks
leaving the sharp reeds.

The last bar of summer
just pretending the geese haven't arrived
bragging butterflies,
and skies of illiterate swifts.

PETER OWEN JONES

ALAN RYCROFT

GREEN JADE BUDDHA

No one even gave him
a second glance—
the Green Jade Buddha
though he's the heart of hosts
who welcomes all
to the kingdom of their lost long
serene nobility;
where being is the ubiquity
of a total hospitality.
No obsequious smiles here
no dollar signs in the till of eyes
no special package to entice
a man out of himself
into exile
from that first Eden
of his innate content.

He was just there standing
almost life size,
—open armed to all
no matter who or what they were—
in the genteel colonial foyer
of Macau's Hotel Lisboa.
Chinese men in a hurry
to get started
on what really matters
make a beeline past him

and the massage parlour.
Their temple and the only god they know
presides over the roulette table
and guides the little spinning ball
towards
(or away from)
the goddess of magnanimous fortune,
the Furies of an unmercied fate.

Pursues them night and day,
and the burning
goes on and on.
They live in a house of fire
with no water
to douse it out.
Tongues that never stop
the murmuring money mantra;
they spin
as they are spun,
turn, as they are turned again
upon the ceaseless
prayer wheel
of desire.

ALAN RYCROFT

EARTH

We walk, we ride, we spit, we stride,
we stomp, we shit, we fight, we glide
over you, almost without a thought
thinking somehow you'd always be there
the mansion of so lordly me
arranged, even divinely ordained, serendipitously.
I was on top of a bus once
and a sunset like a dalai lama
in folds of crimson purple robes, but no one
even raised an eye from their phones —
they'd seen it all a thousand times before.
They live the death of awe.

I had imagined you the victim of us
a mother almost terminally used
and abused by her children of ingratitudes,
grown up as In some dark spell
prodigal and cold, intent only to soar
in technocratic glories
half robot, half man,
to their cyber-immortalities.

But how can I presume to know
who you are?
Who has returned from plummeting
to the bottom of your ocean floor?
or flown with the Condor
over your mountains,
surfed the pure crystalline streams of air?
Who has held fond converse

with the gnomic eloquence of trees?
or dared to hold at once the gaze
of both the tiger and the lamb?
Who has loved as the hoary elephant's
broken heart?
Or penetrated to the part
dolphins play, transmuting light?

Who has walked on lava?
Danced with fire on the volcano
as it blows?
Ridden the wrath of it
to the still core of the rage?
Or stood unbuffeted
in the deep eye of the wind?
Or burrowed down to heavenly hollows
to lost cities and luminous crystal caves,
where only a man who is a buddha can survive?

Earths within earths, worlds within worlds
nested like Russian dolls,
so close, yet so very far from each other.
You are tooth and claw
and the ravening maw
but gentle as you are implacable,
merciful to those of no mercy at all.
But even you have your limits.
You would roar and rile and swallow
those who swarm, gorge and gouge
and burn and poison your pristine.

You're not some poor helpless woman
but a goddess, a mighty queen;

you've space and heart enough
to contain it all, all those who have lived
and died who are nothing but bones and ashes
in your ten million spring embrace:
the kind, the cruel, the generous, mean,
the just and the dishonourable.
You have been bound here with us,
but you will be free.

And parts of you have had their day,
are failing, falling, dying away
as parts of us are failing, falling...
Sometimes it seems like I'm stuck
in a crazy lift plummeting at breakneck speed
through the floors of a collapsing building!
And you are stretching, wakening,
reaching to a further dawn
an unknown sun —
the quickening is on your skin
the touch of a love you never felt before;
as if a new young princely consort
has come to claim last dance with you
to the music of the furthest star.

And the swoon of the embrace.
This pulsation is a presence in all space.
You're no mere whore of Babylon
for bleary eyed bankers, presidents
and the last obscenity of kings to suckle on,
and drink the blood red wine
of the inverted communion
of the priests of the black sun.

And as the Mother is reborn
of light water and light fire
the sons are risen also.
The masks shall be ripped from all faces
to reveal the shadows within
for the time of the dark unleashing is done.
And though I may not live
to see the fullness of the day
the first glimmerings of new dawn is now
and in this garden —
the unspeakable song of our searing,
your death-panged, birthing cry.

ALAN RYCROFT

HENRY SHUKMAN

DAYS OF LIGHT

The rebbe says it's best
not to speak the name
of the dead for seven days.
Let his soul have a break
from being him, before it begins
the trek to a new home.
For these days, he – if it's he –
can be anything at all:
the gargle of the weir,
the sheet of malty water
sliding over the edge,
the froth where it meets
the canal, or the dark elms,
or the tall young heron
bedraggled in its tailcoat.
Released from himself,
creation is all his; he can be
what he was all along:
the cool water, the bright wind,
these seven days of light.

BLESSED

The English word for blessing
is the French word for wound:
blessed or blessé, graced or hurt.
When I saw my father

doubled over at the funeral,
I wondered what dark grace
had taken him like a moth
into the shade of its hands.

The wound needs us to change:
we cannot stay the same.
Forgive me, father,
how much I thought I knew.

HENRY SHUKMAN

DAWN IN GALLUP, NM

The empty lot across the street
is the colour of suede
this last hour before dawn.
You can see it two ways:

houses huddled in the dark trees,
the road with its sheen
under the lamps, all mean
the world of trouble

is still intact, and waiting:
the things you must do, the victories
and defeats: enter
another day of it all.

Or this: that dry ground
no one has wanted,
turning a colour you can't name,
though it has desert in it

and night and somehow water too,
as if the seabed this land once was
can show itself now
in the twilight of dawn,

a ghost of its old condition
remembering the silence
of the ocean.
You can't say why

but there's a hope
in that scrubby abandoned lot,
as if your bones
are friends with it.

Something that matters
is waiting there, something
that one day will make it easier
to die.

Then the light strengthens,
day rouses the trees
to their ordinary colours,
and the empty lot

is just an empty lot.
The first cars drive by,
some with their lights still on,
some not.

HENRY SHUKMAN

FACING THE WALL

It's me and my shadow again,
the little night I cast
on the wall in the room,
looking cubist this morning,
square-shouldered, pin-headed,
neck and skull stretched
into a stalk, while the body
has filled out, a blurred box.
All the trouble, all the
pain, yearning and hope:
all from this one square yard
of darkness on the wall.

Bodhidharma sat this way,
a leaf of a man blown in
from the West, light as dust,
a quaver in the haze,
a blur on the wall,
for whom night and day
were a memory, and life
and death a dream,
who crossed the Yangtse
on a blade of grass,
then planted himself in his cave,
and waited to see
what would grow.

HENRY SHUKMAN

LONDON

That first time he saw her again,
in the big room off Baker Street,
married now, in her leggings
from the Rambert, flushed,
her Jewish frame
alive under the ballet top,
and she smiled at him,
eyes black as olives,
and rose from the sofa,
and made their glasses chime,
a pain like no other
woke in his chest.
He knew what he had to do.
Next day, the phone box.
Then the walking side by side,
fast, her hair fluttering
like feathers in the river breeze.
What are we doing?
Her question hoped for no answer.
In the roar of a train
on the Hungerford Bridge
he reached for her,
and scripture came to life,
she was Bathsheba on the rooftop,
and London grew quiet,
all its motion and fury
powerless to reach them
where they stood holding each other,
at the center of a new temple
only they could see

rising from its ruins,
while a river boat
thrummed beneath them,
moving across the current,
and sent a waft of smoke
up through the girders
beneath their feet.

HENRY SHUKMAN

WIND IN TREES

When trees toss in high wind and a suspicion
of rain travels across their dark faces,
I long for the old summers under smoky oaks.
Whoever I am, it's not who I thought.

Who is it the rain and wind wake with their sighing?
That tree-lover, summer-lover – try and find him,
was he ever there? Did he love? Was he love?
Shh, say the trees, listen closer, listen closer.

HENRY SHUKMAN

GEORGI Y. JOHNSON

BE CURIOUS, THAT RIFTS WILL NOT TEND US

Be curious, my friend,
that rifts will not tend us,
letting absence pattern this blend,
as light flickers through lines
of space and change,
so that borders between us
be intricate webs, waving in beauty
with soft winds of time.

My enemy, be curious.
That I might give you myself,
and be sacrificed to a fire of love
from which this hatred comes.

Be curious, my child,
not to be fooled by ending.
That the distant moon
will stay a miracle.
That each thought and feeling,
each celebration of pain
and wasteland of joy
will keep the doors ajar
to who we truly are.

Curiosity, she is a fire of love
and the end of ignoring.

She is the conscious one,
the source of every sight.

That lets us remember.
That holy care
in being aware.

She is the one.
That burns out fear.
She is awakened.
She is here.

GEORGI Y. JOHNSON

SOOTHING THE INSIDE OUT

A wind chants threads of home,
the wonder of a child within, alone,
an inner creak of sacred bones,
and a dog running nearby.

Can you hear
the silence singing a setting sun?
Listen – this subtle melody
is playing as you.

Colors change in space,
mystery with light in its eyes
through a window – being, seeing
as out there, far away, so close,
a horizon limits sight;
yet curving unseen, sensuous
into these arms, as two hands,
(loyal escorts in happening)
are suddenly now so still,
as if they had shaped the night.

Heat inside flesh and cooler there
Where? Here.
Where this one holds feeling
as contrast to itself,
finding in a vanishing bliss
a great soul behind, before,
timelessly waiting
where hot and cold are one.

Give me a moment of your miracle
Let me come into That universe,
to the sense of what we're meaning to be;
Let's caress this multiple illusion
into emptiness,
where we are always, already free.

GEORGI Y. JOHNSON

ON STRIVING FOR ENLIGHTENMENT

Walking this way, toward that point,
Ahead of us in time and space,
wanting to be "there" – a state of grace,
Never good enough, never good,
not yet there, quite, nearly,
(Oops - it's gone again).

Can you hear the wind whisper?
a loose incantation
as it touches lips and blows through cells?
It's not the wind,
It's you, chanting the stillness.

If you were Buddha now,
the wind would weep,
the water dull, unflavoured
and the earth would miss
the clumsiness
of your weathered shoes.

If you were "there" now,
All holy and unbroken,
you would not be here –
spectacular and human, glittering with the bruises
and open wounds
of all that is alive.

How could we lose
this imperfect mother,
this busy mind,

this warm and sacred
moment of all you were,
all you ever will be
and all you are?

Perfectly pure,
in a grey light of dawn,
where light diffuses
its horizon to the holy dark
in a shower of pristine moments;
each kissing home and still,
caressing space;
gloriously imperfect
in an explosion of awe.

Always here, now,
unceasingly becoming
an endless spiral of love.

GEORGI Y. JOHNSON

WHERE WILL I FIND YOU ?

Where will I find you, my friend?
In an accusing forest of laws,
tortured by stories repented
yet never truly told?

In clear, blameless skies,
before, between and after words,
without verdict, innocent and free,
This is where I find you.

Where will I find you, my love?
Split in shame and disgust
where stinging eyes fame,
the one we could never tame?

In this stainless ocean free
of all monstrosity of fear,
untainted and pure, fiercely alive.
This is where I find you.

Where will I find you my child?
Abandoned in a dark room
where doors slammed shut
as if no-one was there?

Here, I will find you,
in the human moment,
born of infinite, endless care,
where division died before it began.
This is where I find you.

GEORGI Y. JOHNSON

THE LIE THAT YOU ARE GONE

We would have us believe this tree
flowering and bearing sweetest fruit
is the death knell of a seed,
that once entwined with animal fur
found home in fertile soil.

We might see an empire of clouds
reflecting every tincture of light
and decide this transient beauty
is the death chant of a river.

Perhaps we should bow to whispers
that butterflies blown through glories of flowers
are but death knells of caterpillars
we tried to avoid in the mud.

And just as we hear sweet melody, singing
through branches of our minds,
Would we say this song is dying,
even as it is sings?

Does the silent moon decry
the death of a blazing sun?

Always ourselves arriving,
How would we lie and say t
hat now, you have passed?

Is a rock separate from a blade of grass?

Is it liquid, this thin shield of death,
this transparent divider of glass?

Let me in, sweet sister, to your sweetness
Let me dissolve in the nectar of all you are
Let me absorb you into earthly tone
Let it come, let it be, let it be free.

Not grieving but living again
as each step to death
walks us closer to receiving.

GEORGI Y. JOHNSON

IVAN M. GRANGER

TRANSLATIONS

All Adam's offspring form one family tree,
from the beginning, the same life and spirit and quality.

When one limb is bent with pain,
the entire living tree naturally feels the strain.

Thus he indifferent to the agony of another,
cannot be named human alongside his brother.

— SA'ADI

Seeking Truth, I studied religion,
and discovered one single root
        beneath the many branches.

Best, I've found, to be faithless
lest you become lost among the limbs.

Best to find that root, that root that reveals
all meaning and unity,
        clear as day.

— Mansur al-Hallaj

TRANSLATED BY Ivan M. Granger

Steadfast friend,
You have hewn me
        through and through!

When I speak, my every word
        speaks of You.
And when silent,
        silently I ache for You.

— RABIA AL-ADAWIYYA

TRANSLATED BY IVAN M. GRANGER

The fire rises in me,
      and lights up my heart.
Like the sun!
Like the golden disk!
Opening, expanding, radiant—
      Yes!
       —a flame!

I say again:
      I don't know
      what to say!

I'd fall silent
 —If only I could—
but this marvel
      makes my heart leap,
it leaves me open mouthed
      like a fool,

urging me
      to summon words
      from my silence.

—SYMEON THE NEW THEOLOGIAN

TRANSLATED BY IVAN M. GRANGER

All in azure today
was my queen—here, before me—
My heart hammered with sweet delight,
and in rising streams
my soul was lit with silent light.
But in the distance, burning down,
the fierce earth fire smoked from the ground.

— VLADIMIR SOLOVIEV

TRANSLATED BY IVAN M. GRANGER

BENT

Yes, seekers, do
sit up,
stand tall.

But hear
my bent secret:

       All saints slouch.

God's lovers lean
into the divine embrace
and there
let the years pass.

       Struggling for straightness,
       your strivings shaken,

       learn what true knowers know:

Effort clears the way,
but the steps
are already taken.

IVAN M. GRANGER

WHEN THE SPRING THAW COMES

Something they
won't tell you —

That book of sins
you hide
beneath your pillow
matters
not at all.

When the spring thaw comes
we all go mad
and shred it,
tossing love notes
left and right
scribbled on the scraps.

IVAN M. GRANGER

MIRABAI STARR

MOTHER OF GOD, SIMILAR TO FIRE

Mother of God
similar to fire,
ignite my heart in prayer.
Where once I stood on familiar ground,
selecting my spiritual experiences
like choice morsels from a well-tended larder,
now my garden has gone up in flames
and I thirst only for the Living God.
Let me find him, Mother,
as you do,
deep inside my own ripened being.
Let me swallow the Sacred
and burn with that Presence,
illuminating a way home to the Truth.
Lit from within,
let my blazing heart become a sanctuary
for the weary traveler,
until this long night lifts
and dawn unfolds her new radiance.

CENACLE OF THE NEW PENTECOST

Mother of God,
you are the safe haven,
the secret room where the lovers of the Divine
gather to remember him,
the oasis where the seekers find each other
in the heart of the desert
and exchange stories of longing and discovery.
The fire of the Holy Spirit
comes pouring into the open chamber of your mother-heart. In
your midst, all are welcome.
Through your voice, everything is understood.
Blessed Mother,
may all faiths find sanctuary in you.
May all paths flow like mountain streams
into the river-valley of your love
and praise the Holy One
with a thousand voices.

MIRABAI STARR

MOTHER OF GOD, SHE WHO HEARS THE CRIES OF THE WORLD

for Andrew Harvey

Mother of Mercy,
the cries of the world keep me awake at night.
I rise from my bed, but I cannot locate the source of the wailing.
It is everywhere, Mother, coming from all directions,
and my heart is shattered by the sheer intensity of suffering. You
of boundless compassion,
expand my heart so that I can contain the pain.
Focus my mind so that I can arrive at viable solutions,
and energize my body so that I can engage in effective action.
Give me the courage to follow the crumbs of heartbreak
all the way home to the place where I can be of real service.
Let me dip my fingers into the dew of your compassion
and scatter it now over the fevered brow of this world.

MIRABAI STARR

THE HOLY PROTECTION OF THE MOTHER OF GOD

Mother of Mercy,
if I stay awake all night,
vigilant and grateful,
will you drop your protective veil
over my vulnerable heart?
I cannot control the world around me;
I can only be faithful to my own deepest truth.
Wrap me in your pure white cloak of devotion, Mary,
so that I can remember that my sole task
is to praise the God of Love.
Cover me in your burial shroud
as I die to my false self,
to be reborn
as a living example of peace on earth.
Infuse me with the tincture of your tears,
so that I may face every challenge
with a tender and courageous spirit.

MIRABAI STARR

THE MOTHER OF GOD MAGADAN

Broken-hearted,
open-hearted,
brave-hearted Mother of God,
I weep with you.
You take into your arms
those who have given up everything for the Truth.
All over the world,
throughout the ages and right now,
the blood of the martyrs is spilled:
in prison camps and inner cities,
on battlefields and in hospitals,
in churches and synagogues and mosques;
they bleed for justice for the voiceless,
for peace on earth,
for the freedom to praise,
for the rights of all beings to live in dignity;
they bleed for the bleeding earth.
And you, Blessed Mother,
receive them all and weep for them.
Each one is your own holy child.
Each sacrifice is a sword in your own heart.

MIRABAI STARR

IRINA KUZMINSKY

HOMAGE TO EMILY DICKINSON

And if –
That Silence were – a Ruse –
So we should look – away
And if –
The Mystery – which grows
In the heart's night – should herald – day
If –
There was something – being prepared
And sacrifice was – needed
Would I then understand – the Cross
And all – It – holds – within it?
If –
I were ready to – accept
The price to make – All – sacred
And not – to cling and not – to fear
When told – the Game – was ended –
Would I then understand – the Tomb
And not seek to – transcend it
But let Transcendence come – at will
And meet – the One – who Made it –

SHE RIDES

Let me pierce the awakening shroud
with tiger's tendrils
The lady rides

When Glauke's face peers from Medea's robes
and Glauke burns and then still burns
The lady rides

When yakshinis, rusalkas, willis dance
their tree limbs, water shifts enflowed, entwined
The lady rides

When tigers, lions, hyenas, jackals, hounds
lithely stampede and crush the tender grass
The lady rides

When brothers murder brothers for a different face
and rain falls acidly on ghostly trees
The lady rides

When air which carries poison mocks our lungs and eyes
while cherries blossom flagrantly in yards close by
The lady rides

When solid earth sends out a deeper groan
and those whose bodies listen start to toss and turn
The lady rides

She rides
She rides
As wells give up their dead

She rides
She rides
As mountains rear a stallion's head

Her necklaces will clatter in the night
A lassoo sings and whines in flight
The flanks of all wild things are goaded
Till they gnash and bite
She rides
When stars in dancing frenzy dip into the sea
and Hokusai waves rise perfect to their welcome – Then
The lady rides
When Francis preaches to the birds
and Rumi turns and turns in search of Shams
The lady rides
While Hafiz sing the praise of wine
and Nizam shows El-Arabi her face
The lady rides

We're dervishes – and
pierce the shroud
– and mad
awakening
with love's
sharp tendrils
tiger mounted
The lady rides.

IRINA KUZMINSKY

GROUND ZERO

I know that somewhere
Every thought exists
I know that somewhere
My desires have taken form
I know that somewhere
This side of the abyss
No love I've lived
Has ever yet been lost—

I know the pattern is complete
When I have glimpsed it from beyond
I know the pieces interlock
Where each sound comes to its own place—

I know we two between us have
Infinity
Of time Of space
And, late or soon, two halves must meet,
And in their joining refind Grace—

I know all this—
But my thirst still persists—
And I am caught in the dark cloud
Between Eternity and Time

What choice have I
But to allow the waters of the deep abyss
To cleanse the last dregs
From my clinging mind?
I ache to know not knowing

Laugh fall weep
I ask to be unbound
To be met and to meet
I want to touch ground zero
Caught by Your heady scent
And slip – small salamander –
Through the netting of the web
Then wait that You should catch me
In the fragrance of Your lap.

IRINA KUZMINSKY

RABIA MAGDALENA

Rabia magdalena
There is no shame
And every lover
Brings you closer
To the Lover –
When you learn
How to look.

Rabia magdalena
There is an openness
Which leads straight to the Lover's arms
And even treading dark paths of desire
How could you lose your way?

Rabia magdalena
You took the shortest path
And learned to love
All that you once had feared.
Straight as a flaming arrow
Was your path –
It burnt through all remorse.

O Rabia magdalena!
Freed by the heart of Love
You – Alchemist –
Made impure pure
And degradation grace.

O Rabia magdalena!
I have read:

By passion is this world bound
And through passion it's released
You yielded passion-filled to love
In every guise your Lover took
And found void, fullness, peace and grace
Within the open secret of your Lover's arms.

IRINA KUZMINSKY

HAGAR I & II

Sands, sands
Submerge me not

Wasteland
Show me your wells

Water of life
Living water I need
If this child
If I am to live

Fugitive am I
Fleeing from servitude
Death in the wilderness
Beckons
Better I die as I seek my true home
Than eat the bread of contrition

Tent of my master
You brought me a child
Tent where my master's wife led me
And yet my master was not unkind
And I could scarcely bear leave him

Seize me in ecstasy
Seize me in glory
Lost in the desert I perish
Tumbleweed blown
So far from home
A wanderer
I am weeping

IRINA KUZMINSKY

You are El-roi
The One Who Sees Me

Trembling
Tumbling
Inwards
Vertigo
Threatens
My mind

Desert winds
Heard
Of my wandering
I ask
The sands
To be kind

You
Who can witness
My suffering
You
Are the Lord
Of my life
Your name is
The One Who Sees Me
And I've seen God
Still alive

—Am I—
... I am

IRINA KUZMINSKY

THE PURE ARE HARD-PRESSED TO PERCEIVE WHAT IS IMPURE

The pure are hard pressed to perceive what is impure
For in their observation alchemy is found
Transforming objects of perception through their gaze
For is it not said that these two —
The gaze and what is gazed upon —
Are One?

What is perceived cannot exist without the organ of
                                                        perception
And just as atoms can't decide if they are waves
(we must decide for them instead)
So does the Light which looks through guileless eyes
Cleanse and transform what its ray touches.

IRINA KUZMINSKY

EPIPHANY

Epiphany is light
No crushing Presence
But a look
Which pierces with its kindness

This love which sees all, knows all
Yet still loves
Calls forth that Love
Which looked inside each living creature
At its birth

IRINA KUZMINSKY

IN THE BEGINNING

In the beginning was the Word
But Silence Was
Before every Beginning—

Therefore, my soul,
Be still—and smile into the Silence
If you would know
The Origin of Light.

IRINA KUZMINSKY

JENNY D'ANGELO

SAVED

I see it when I prepare food.
Chopping vegetables or pouring out grains of rice
I see how I watch the pieces that get left out
or the grains that fall away from the pot.
I always pick them up.
Taking the extra effort to wash them again
if they've landed on the floor or the counter top,
I put them back in the pan or the soup.
And always I think of the biblical story:
The great Lord God talking
about who will live and who will die
in Sodom and Gomorrah.
Abraham asks, "If I can find fifty righteous people,
will you destroy the whole city?"
Then finally coming down to
"What about one good person —
will you destroy the whole place if I can find one good soul?"

I always think of that and save the grain of rice.
Saying this one has come so far, grown with all the others, come
finally to my kitchen, in my hand,
and now I have dropped it. So I rescue the one grain or bean.

Thinking always if someone saw me,
I would also be rescued.

When I am reminded
who I truly am —

I am the cook.
I am the water.
I am the pot.
I am the bean
finally seen and savored.

JENNY D'ANGELO

BEYOND ALL SEEABLE PROOF

What is deeper than want and wider than fear?
The heart of a human, capable and free.

Beyond the sensing of now and then,
further from the noise and tumult,
there is the truth of love.

The unending connection
with the great source of it all.
Not some old man in the sky
but the huge, vast Oneness.

Divine Mother, some say.
I can take away the holy names
and still keep the nearness
of her embrace

because I experience it here.
It is in a newborn's eyes.
It is in the hummingbird's wings
tuned to infinity.

When we share our naked hearts,
even those hard nuggets of hollow doubt
from the black night, we are cracked open,
and for more than just ourselves.

The unspoken seeking is answered
by us together. Quietly and so personally

we add to the collective good
by our words, facing the storm.

JENNY D'ANGELO

BRUSH LOADED WITH LIGHT

Looking at your picture, you are still radiant with light.
Now I remember how it was at the end—
your cheeks so sunken, your skin
so tight across the bones.

We all saw your eyes.
We saw the light that emanated out from you.
Even people who do not believe they can see angels
saw the light from you.

We saw the peace that was with you.
You kept giving it out to us,
the light you were and the peace you were—
somehow the same.

My pen may not be able to load itself with light
but I am writing you in it anyway.
You are precious in my heart and now
after all the days of sadness, I begin to linger again
in your kindness and your grace.

If there is any light in me, it is
what was close to you, what was like you,
what is like us all. In the end it is only Light.

JENNY D'ANGELO

THE FRAGILE OPENNESS

Maybe you know it from sex
or from birth or from prayer.

That fragile sliver of time
when you know everything.

You know who you are. And
you know your place in the world.

This is really all you ever need to know.
Everything else falls from it.

Learn to trust that breath,
that instant, that touch, that glance.

Not exaggerating. Not rushing.
Just having it fully.

JENNY D'ANGELO

TODAY IS SUCH A DAY

It is again the first day of joy.
Always it feels like freshness—a ground spring
running sparkling and cool—to be here.
This is a secret water in which we flow,
a special location in the universe
where the heart is allowed to be,
open and free, ruthless and tender.

I trust in this with all my being
and this trust rolls back on itself
to feed me light. I can feel
the light entering, enduring,
like the breeze, like the stars.

All these shining miracles live in us.
So I allow the rumbling murmurations,
sparkling catches of light. Following
them is like following my own breath.

Following, leading, stumbling, flying
all seem to be in the same web and fibre
and expanse. All seem blessed on this day,
when the wind is perfect.

If I am veering only to light, then so be it.
All the edges of sight are layered in light.
This is what I follow.
Call it heart. Call it peace.
Incomprehensible and full of beauty.
Call it now.

JENNY D'ANGELO

INSIDE A STONE

What love is it in the inside of a stone?

Have you ever known one stone or rock
so well you could find it blindfolded,
amongst a pile on the table?

It is a revelation. This one stone —
maybe came from the Arctic or
Greenland or Japan. Maybe it
rolled all along the ocean bottom
to land on your beach.

Maybe it was shattered from a glacier
or spewed out from fire-pouring volcano.
Maybe this one stone is part of the heart
of Gaia. Maybe Gaia came to you today
in this very piece of herself.

Then you can begin to wonder if these grains
of sand are the offspring of this stone.
All connected? All once one mass?
Impossible to know.

But the possibility opens you
to the web of life again.

Great Teachings say we are all connected.
If you can feel this from the holding of a stone,
one stone, then maybe the Earth is
one surface of graceful growing and we are

the grateful holders of her, our Mother,
whom we bless by holding even such a stone
in our keen hands.

JENNY D'ANGELO

HARVEY & RAMSAY

DIANA DURHAM

NEW ENGLAND NIGHT

The over-arching figures of the stars
glittered in completeness as the true dark
deepened in a clear, open country night.

The blue covering sky was gone with the sun
dissolved into this vast black diamanté dome—
but that word reflects our Earth-shaped thought—

This perspective is not painted on
an antique ceiling: those stars are small
because of unimaginable distance.

Some may no longer even exist
their light still travelling
towards us; all light passageways of thought

to help us comprehend still further depths
of still more stars not visible from here.
Every night we live with this open-

Ended space above our heads: to be
vulnerable to the nakedness
of night is to grasp something about

Ourselves: an unimaginable depth
the timeless presence of the dark,
the great silence of constellations.

FATHER OF NIGHT

A presence is flowing towards me
out of the dark tonight

plentiful, endlessly

as endless as the road
that sweeps up to us
feeds itself
endlessly endlessly
under the car

this road is not beautiful
but it could also be
a way this radiance
pours itself out
into the night

the purple grey shades
of steel girdered bridges
neon-lit, white-lit
the giant bones
of overpasses
passing and repeating
sometimes the road
is faintly star-lit.

The black pours towards us
seamlessly

in branches and wide grey
stretches of flat river

the dark-rayed continuous
outpouring of its giant
movement steady
into the evening
that we are moving in now.

Simply like water
like black air
or the soft trajectories
of night rain
blown horizontal by the wind
or our rushing against
its silent wet softness

the presence of what we always dreamed
or never noticed
all the ways that we were always held
in this embrace.

DIANA DURHAM

DETOUR

Is that a road to anywhere? The sun's
great gold ball waiting at the end, spilling
gold down its broken asphalt, at the turn
the sign says Detour, where is it going?

This side, the shambolic trees of winter,
tips edged red with fire, penned in like unruly
spectators behind the chain link border
on the other, left over huts, poorly

developed zonings, new office build half planned
these are the strange lands, are they the wastelands
that fall between our seeing? I want to see
the way the sun does, so excitedly

glowing as if this detour, forgotten
scrap of town led to the door of heaven.

DIANA DURHAM

SEE CLEAR THROUGH TO THE SUN

well I understand now how beauty is a flow
that springs invisibly but is fed by all things
how transparency is first, and what glass would bring,
and how all its words must be constantly renewed,
cleaned of obligations from their careless past.
To speak simply is to be this complex embrace,
reclaim the headwaters, pass through the liquid face
soften in the wet darkness my hardening gaze
and see inside the pitted surface was my own.
With it dissolves bitterness, irritation
the perplexed disappointment of looking without
finding, so that feeling moves out away from doubt
and I know because this beauty flows that it can
take form. And therefore all we have to do is plan
a temple to it—these lines may begin some part
of its foundation—whatever can impart
a benediction, the only way we ever
build what we love, when this spills easily over
and that space out there, those hills, the tower and town
square, become the place that matches, catches and turns
back through us its meaning, like sunlight on canyon
walls, like faces we can see clear through to the sun.

DIANA DURHAM

THE MASS

We are listening to a tapestry
woven entirely from air, moving cloth
of sound purer even than spun gold
its stories advance in tumbling symmetries

and process through the hall, as the layers
ascend, drop down, embrace — each threaded piece
fine cast from the complex loom of players.
In the honey gold dimmed light, gilt relief

panels soar like doorways to a palace,
on the bright stage starry hosts are singing
differently altogether, voicing
the mass. Sanctus, sanctus, we acquiesce

sated, full, incandescent with the mass,
all our lives woven with the light of us.

After hearing Bach's Mass in B Minor
sung by the Cantata Singers at Jordan Hall, Boston

DIANA DURHAM

CHRIS SAADE

UNRELENTING FREEDOM CARVES MY SOUL

You, Life, mysterious and abundant,
are the unbending urge for freedom within me —
to be free, to live free,
to remain unshackled,
unburdened from self-hate and self-doubt.

Free to become the body that I am.
free to wear the spirit that bears my name,
Free to walk proud,
bowing my head to no dictates,
other than the invitation to love.

May I, in my freedom,
continue to love passionately,
to seek peace for all,
and to stand compassionately for justice.

Today I offer gratitude for the call to love's freedom.
I praise the sacred freedom that is the essence of life.
I praise the unrelenting freedom that carves my soul,
repeatedly assigns dignity to my heart,
and sheer beauty to my existence !

I CELEBRATE THE DEFEATS I HAVE KNOWN

Let me hold as holy, O God,
the defeats that have enriched my journey.
I am learning from You, O God,
that for the freedom of my spirit and all spirits,
I can endure the soul's fight.
I can bless the times of manifestation
and the times of loss,
the times of rejoicing
and the times of disappointment.
I can, through it all,
let my passion remain my prayer.

I know that the journey toward love is sacred
in all its ebbs and flows.
In Your presence
I celebrate the defeats I have known.
When I was broken,
my heart kept praying,
kept caring, seeking, and learning.
And these times were holy.

There are lesions
that a heart that refuses to shut down,
has to endure—
wounds to be offered at the altar of love.
These wounds are precious in Your eyes, O God,
You who see our struggles
and partake in our striving.
Blessed be Your name,
always and forever.

CHRIS SAADE

TEACH US HOW TO SPEAK JUSTICE

O You, who see beyond our seeing,
O You, who are in love with our spirits,
You, who are the signature of the timeless within our souls,
Teach us how to love without limits.

Teach us how to speak justice with the passion of our longing
and let a great strength be born in us from our sisters' and
                                    brothers' tears.

Let us always revere Your vision of justice
and pray without ceasing.

For You are within us—the heart, the longing, and the prayer.
You are the ineffable demands of love within and without.
May we remain faithful to the limitless aspirations of Your
                        sacred heart.

                                        CHRIS SAADE

HARVEY & RAMSAY

PHILIP WELLS

THE STORM OF CREATION

Thunder –
two continents
of rock collide.

Lightning –
a crack
in the eggshell sky.

Rain –
cleansing
for the sacrifice.

She cuts off your mind
with a golden sword

and to the drum
of the infinite drum

you hatch
in the healing moss;

and dried
by the lovelight of suns

you fly out beyond
the outer skies

to explode
your star of love,

sending out
the storm of your seed

to wake new wings
to the highest skies of fire.

PHILIP WELLS

HALLOWED GROUND

Can truth, like jewels, be suddenly found?
In a dream the words lit up my mind:
To ignite the fellowship of hallowed ground.

What does it mean, this eerie sound?
Is it Time itself I hear unwind?
Can truth, like jewels, be suddenly found?

Our planet-threads will fray, unwound;
My task, perhaps, to weave and bind,
To ignite the fellowship of hallowed ground:

One day to see the teachers crowned,
The wheelchairs walk, the killers kind:
Can truth, like jewels, be suddenly found?

Our star shines still as we go round –
From that vast flame the spark I'll find
To ignite the fellowship of hallowed ground.

In storms of mind we run aground;
To the stellar wind still blinkered, blind.
Truth will, like jewels, be suddenly found
To ignite the fellowship of hallowed ground.

PHILIP WELLS

LINES FROM ASSISI

We have come not to shout, but to listen;
Not to hoard, but to share;
Not to lash out, but to calm;
Not to cover up, but to lay bare.

We have come not to suffocate, but to touch;
Not to dictate, but to understand;
Not to hold back, but to unleash –
Not to shrink, but to expand.

We have come not to shadow, but to colour;
Not to conquer, but to embrace;
Not for ourselves, but for the other –
Not to silence, but to give voice.

PHILIP WELLS

VISITOR

A poem is a dream of sound and this is my dream:
I dream of a vast sunbird from Andromeda
Gliding to our planet on the secret
Thermal breath of stars.
The sunbird lands on Madagascar
In a frenzied din of hope and fear.
From the cavern of its ear, a figure descends –
Thin and graceful as an impala;
Its cloak of feathers the colours of fire.
The face is almost human, but shines like a wetsuit.
The eyes are stiller and deeper than a whale's.

In the clash of cameras, Earth's great leader
Swells with bearded charisma and points to the sky.
His top scientists have lassoed the moon
And are winching it across for an eclipse, so their visitor
May observe the entire planet lit up by day in neon light.
The visitor takes the leader's hand and hushes him
With his sea-dark eyes. "Please do not," the visitor whispers.
"Please take me to the edge of your sea, to a place
Where only the wind and the waves disagree."
A young scientist with nocturnal eyes knows a place.
"By the desert. The Skeleton Coast."

The young man takes them there and under the first stars
The three men sit crosslegged in the sand,
Looking out at the skeletons of battered ships,
Listening to the tale of the wind and the waves.
"In your loud world" the visitor begins, "I must tell you this."
"The knowledge that will save you lives in sound. All the

love,

The truth of happiness: all is hidden in natural sound."

Wave after wave falls in the night.

"But what about silence?" the young man asks.

"The greatest secrets of all are hidden
In the ultrasound of silence.
The power that fuels the brightest stars burns there."

"But what must we do?" the leader asks.

"We shall wait patiently for the dawn—
And listen to the songs of the light."

PHILIP WELLS

THE REVOLUTION OF REVELATIONS

Petals squeezed down the barrels of Kalashnikovs was OK —
But the long division of insurrection's due for correction:
Desperate times call for inspiration out of time, a holy way
To shine the bigbang prayer of the burningsane expansion —

And so recitations of reciprocity erupt with unprecedented
ferocity
And the veracity of capacity hearts is the start
Of the end of verbosity; and the festival of light — in cities
And towns spreads from candle to candle, from heart

To heart — and we can hear the end of fear burning
In the turning spheres of sacred tears of falling light;
Too subtle for sense and tense, but second sighting
And the sounding light of it is true — the truth of light —

The time to fight is now; for all those guards to fall…
Bulldozing of the final wall! Asleep no more…
We are too bright, too tall, to fall again, too tall
Now we have shrunk upon our knees and score

The rhythmical heat of the heart of ourselves.
Pills we never knew left on darkened shelves
We take now and score the kick of who we truly are:
O holy ghost, you superstar! Never knew how far

The sky stretched through the old bars of who
I thought I was, who I bought I was, the stealing
Of my feelings, little thoughts of me in charge but no —
Now I am the feeling sky breathing round the world your
healing.

PHILIP WELLS

DANCE OF THE DARK GODDESS

She's calling you.
Yes you.

She's calling you home,
whispering sweet somethings in your ear.

Can you hear Her?

She's the song of Love,
the dance of Death,
the fire of Truth.

In the dark night of your Soul
when you're writhing in agony
and there's nowhere to turn
and nothing left to do,
it's time.

Time to surrender your feet to Her fire.
Time to dance in the flames of Her destruction.
Time to burn
burn
burn
in the heart of Her crucible,
and offer it all
to the pyre of Her love.

And when there's nothing left of you, save ash
She'll pause for a moment

and bow Her head in silence.
Not in mourning,
but to savour the sweetness of you,
your life
and your death.
The death of who you thought you were.

And then slowly
She'll lift Her head
with a glint in her eyes
and that wicked knowing smile.
And She'll gather her skirt
and kick up Her heels
and dance wildly on your ashes.

She'll whoop and holler Her incantations of old
breathing new life into your Soul,
summoning you,
commanding you
to rise
rise
rise again.

And you do.

LISA PAGE

I DON'T KNOW

Let us drown
in the tears of our longing.

Let us burn
in the fire of our desires.

Let us be blown away
by the unfathomable mystery
that has brought us
to this very moment
of inevitable liberation,
as we rise up
into the depths
of who we are.

Some call this Love.
Some call it Freedom.
Some call it Consciousness.

I don't know
what to call it.
Perhaps I never will.

But call it
I do.

Again
and again
and again.

It is what I live for.

It is,
as far as I can see,
the only reason we are here.

LISA PAGE

FOOLISH GAMES

Oh my Beloved,

why do we play this game of seek, and hide
the very gifts we come to bare?

How I ache for your bounty,
just as you long for mine.

Let us not waste any more time
with foolish games.

It wears down my soul
and breaks my heart
with every moment that goes unplundered.

If we are to play this game of hide and seek,
then let our 'count to ten' be now.

Let this be the moment,
of our most urgent
declaration,
'Ready or not, here I come!',
as we take each other by the hand,
and dive naked
into the Fire of Love
from which we will never return the same.

LISA PAGE

PETIT MORT

This little death we seek
in a hurried
flurry
of bodies
rubbing together
for sexual pleasure
is just a taste,

of the agonising ecstasy
that awaits us
in every
given moment,

if only we would
passionately embrace our own life,
thrusting ourselves
into each new moment,
over and over again
until we surrendered open
to our own claim
bursting into ecstatic revelation
of death into an ever new life.

LISA PAGE

SAID SHE

Said She,
the Mother of Darkness
and Keeper of the Light.

"When the sun sinks
into oblivion
pouring darkness
over your waking life,
fear not.

That is when I come
to set your Soul on Fire
so that you can
dance in the dark
radiantly alight
as the Love you Are."

LISA PAGE

HELEN MOORE

THE KNIFE

They have made me
a knife—

not a weapon,
but a tool to handle
their expectation,
judgment,
the rough bark
of commands
the moral platitudes
they'd crowd
in dull acidic soil.

They have made me
a tempered blade

to whittle Life
down to its green fibres,
to cleave a staff of clarity,
with which to stand
witness to the rain,

the woods
my naked truth—

they have made me
a cutting
edge.

DEEP TIME, DEEP TISSUE

for L.

Here on the altar to multi-dimensional experience
I'm prostrate and naked (from the waist veiled
with a towel), face ensconced in a leatherette crescent
through which I may disappear

    Your fingers beginning cool, now radiate the Sun
    into layers of dermis, subcutaneous fat
    towards the deeper muscle, at first following the grain
    working with awareness, a mental

    Gray's Anatomy (all red-raw & flayed!) and your honed
    sense of intuition. Slowly, where your deft hands
    press, my body's armour is assuaged – those knots
    tight as rivets, these flat metallic plates

    tensioned as if to snap, these blades tempered
    bands of steel. Time expanding and warmth in oily
                           kneading
    start to release the stress and toxins, which life
    in the Anthropocene engenders in our being

        *

Much later I'll sob like a child
a stream of dammed emotion gushing out
which left me feeling lighter, as if
I really had shouldered a burden

    But for now I float – am foetus

deep sea mammal
first bubble of life
in some primordial lagoon

This aching body that at times
I've hated, softens as its contours roll
this body formed from dust of stars

(ah, the energy rippling through us now!)

Deep time, deep tissue –
eyes form black holes. Sometimes I'm dark matter
drawing everything towards me, swallowing it in
(the way Nut swallows the Sun)
making follicles, cells, poems

This 'me' rapidly collapsing, this 'me'
a mere speck, a gleam in Time's eye
yet developed and refined
over millions of years
by our symbiotic planet

*

Earth, our home that awed
our brave-new astronauts –

wild, animate planet
set in cosmic velvet –

inestimable worth, curves
drifting blue and white

*

O, Anthropocene
period of consequences –

    in a pinch of geological time our minds
    have made deserts of grasslands

    dead-zones in oceans, have cut away
    vast sections of rainforest 'lung'

    erasing cultures of birds, animals, people
    eroding soils elaborated for millennia

    We knowing humans
    disrupting the grand cycles

    of biology, chemistry, geology, knowingly persist
    in filling the atmosphere with gases

    which trap the Sun's rays
    melting glaciers, turning seas acidic

    and where our ice-sheets melt
    prospect for yet more of Gaia's bitter blood.

O, obscene era
this is an emergency!

       *

We breathe, releasing the enormity
of this awareness. How I love

    and thank you, dearest Body! You
    ancient, four-zoaed temple

open to the skies and aligned to Polaris –
hub around which all other stars

    wheel. In whatever mortal span
    that remains, help me to navigate

this crisis in our evolution, to stay
with what others have begun

    millions of antibodies rising
    in and for our life-source, Earth

willing Ecozoa's birth

H ELEN M OORE

Note:

The current geological epoch, named the Holocene, encompasses the growth and impacts of industrial civilisation on our planetary ecosystems. Given these impacts, which have global significance for the future evolution of all living species, a new term 'Anthropocene' was proposed in 2000 by Paul Crutzen & Eugene Stoermer to denote the present time interval. However, critics say that this overstates and reinforces a human-centred perspective, and deprives us of an inspiring vision for a new ecological age. My neologism 'Ecozoa' encapsulate this, and references Blake's 'Four Zoas'.

SPACED OUT

It was a close-run thing   wasn't it?
I mean, watching you   a century from now

     ensouled, emplaced, engaged

in outloving/outwitting the colonists   (spiritual warrior)
their limitless horizons   expanding   in all directions
claiming space   towers & spires
needling   the clouds
uprooting humans   forests, animals, plants
the wild preserved in nominal enclosures

     Cuckoo Lane, Primrose Hill

their fantasy inventing ever new   frontiers
till Gaia had been girdled   with this homogenous project

     ('scientific materialism')

And   in   their   privileging of Reason
they'd become so un-reasonable   that for a while
we disembodied beings

     (awaiting our next incarnation)

feared our projected future –   spaced out
   like prisoners   inside blank-eyed pods & capsules
floating colonies of limbs   amputated from home

     no Lilac-scent, no birdsong, no salt-rush of ocean

And o, how we willed you, early 21st century humans

to draw on your courage, your wildest hopes & visions
your faith in the ultimate blessings of service   to withstand
their torture, their desecration!

> *Did you sense how sometimes we'd lean in, rebalance*
> *your feet, or that we'd speak… (those rare, but shattering*
> *voices)?*

> *How we'd lead you to open that email/weblink*
> *at that synchronous moment*

> *how we'd cross your path with silvery insistence*
> *pointing the way?*

Of course you laboured mostly in the dark
but occasionally you'd see the Moon eclipse
a skyscraper   glinting beside it

Sometimes you felt so small, so a t o m i s e d
your mind encased in iron – no, you couldn't possibly secure
humanity's survival   alone!

But already millions were rising right around the globe
and linking up you led each other
towards a distant speck of light – that portal through which
thanking you – *our wise, brave ancestors* – with shrieks & wails
we'd enter the world   would grow

> One century on   we thrive in woody folds
> flowering fields and Gorse-clad dunes.
>> Look, our forests have been replanted and the seas
>> are gradually receding….

HELEN MOORE

THOMAS R. SMITH

AT THE LINCOLN MEMORIAL

It has taken me sixty-two years
to arrive at this place belonging to
every American. Sixty-two years
in which this marble colossus has remained
diminished in photos. (It's taken as long
to discover the tiny Lincoln ghosted
among the penny's columns.) Meanwhile has our
country's dream also become a phantom?

My immigrant German grandfather
so admired Lincoln he pasted clippings
of the Memorial into his prized
volume of the great liberator's
writings. When his daughter, my mother,
was born, the Memorial still under
construction, he must have dreamt of someday
making the pilgrimage to Washington.

Not within a small-town Lutheran pastor's
means, though fortunately within mine.
I've come to stand for us both in this space,
strangely vast, dominated by the presence
of that gargantuan man, so pale against
the greying walls of history, gravely solitary
above the surging waves of tourists. Such large
hands you have, O Captain! Your taut knuckles

say nearly as much of your resolve
as the straight-ahead determination

of your gaze. Irrespective of size,
this is a Lincoln you wouldn't want to
get in the way of. And the massive right
foot perched forward, as if he could pull
himself up, rise again at any moment—
no wonder so many, after his death

on Good Friday, half-believed in a Christ—
like second coming of him, elevated
by his martyrdom to mythic redeemer,
who, like King Arthur for the Britons,
might in some future crisis return
to save the nation. If America's
true religion is democracy, and if
that religion has a temple, this is it.

Does that faith live on past our "mystic chords
of memory"? In a time when mis-aimed
anger might tear the temple down, I too
call on the railsplitter to wake. Anguish also
in this place consecrated to hope, and
nearby in the black pages of that stone book
burying us alive in names, and down
the Mall, where Powhatan's trail of tears leads straight

to the Capitol steps . . . This dream of
a republic, either it means something
or it doesn't. If it has truth, it belongs
to everyone. If not, all of this is nothing
but a pile of lies, betrayals, corpses.
Was it worth it? What is it worth to us now
to lose or carry on? America, we can't
have it both ways. We'll have to decide.

note: Busboys and Poets Restaurant, Washington DC - above "Detroit on this side, Toledo on the other" (Delta flight attendant), October 6, 2010

THOMAS R. SMITH

JULIA BUTTERFLY HILL

She sacrificed years of her youth on the ground
to perch at one hundred and fifty feet,
outlasted storms, loneliness, sickness, cold,
decisively defeated fear, learned
to draw spiritual strength directly
from the heart of a giant redwood tree.

Pacific Lumber Company money men
tried tempting her with deceptive offers,
when that failed, murderous harassment:
she resisted, for over seven hundred
days and nights did not fall, but stayed
balanced on her aerial platform.

She wept often, and prayed often, and
did not come down. Killers raged the sky
around her, fires and chainsaws menaced,
sometimes she lay in pain and delirium
high above the clear-cuts and burning
yet still did not descend from her purpose.

One must learn to be a lung breathing in smoke,
a swollen-shut eye that sees clearly,
a frostbite-blackened hand that holds on,
a voice heard over helicopter winds,
a spirit able to kick away the scaffolding
of faith and trust the wings it supported,

one must learn these things to do what she did.

THOMAS R. SMITH

DARKNESS FALLING

The small and large things we desired
and denied ourselves or could not have,
that burned so brightly in our minds,
are turning to bits of darkness in air.

They fall and slowly cover the ground,
their darkness becoming the earth
that deepens around us, in which the strange
night-flower of our unlived life grows.

THOMAS R. SMITH

BODIES

'each body a lion of courage'
—*Mary Oliver*

I saw clearly that each person
is a different way of being in
a body. Each a different solution
to the problem of being male or female,
black or white. The weak, the strong,
the beautiful and those who break down
under stress of keeping this clay lamp
lit with beauty. Each soul different,
each charged with maintaining, relating
to its earthly vessel. Each springing from
seed, curving up from the ground of its
possibility, each bowing again at its
final limit to return itself and its
gifts to the Giver. Each a "lion
of courage," each flesh, no matter how
imperfect, distorted, or neglected,
a hero. Each a visible signature
in matter, unlike another. Each admirable,
each to be loved, each when it arrives
to be welcomed, each when it leaves to be
sung home. Each, no matter how inscrutably,

an expansion of being beyond my own,
a surging farther out from my shoreline
of the tide of existence. Each my kindred
dust granted upright mobility and
clothed in the promise and glory of living,
each marked and recorded by its Author,
the motives of all understood and
sympathized with, all struggles and unseen
nobilities noted, the desires of all,
no matter how foolish appearing to
the cold onlooking eye, respected,
seen, honored, and lovingly blessed by an
Inside which knows no outside.

THOMAS R. SMITH

DARKNESS DISEASE

We dismiss the images at our peril:
in the Sunday paper's ads for games, *Doom*
and *Assassin's Creed*. Muscle-armored
drab of the downtown theater's poster
X-Men: Apocalypse, a battle-
bulked figure contemplating a Yorick-
like skull: *Only the Strong Will Survive*.

Only, we rationalize, entertainment,
but the subterranean truth of these
ubiquitous displays is that our gun-
deaths and never-ending war have become
a cancer on our soul, a Darkness
Disease killing our will not only to
keep ourselves alive but the planet.

Each empire carries the seed of
its destruction. I know that this rage
we secretly turn inward on ourselves
is telling us to die. Let's release our dream
of redemptive violence and give
the heroes peace, call the armies home.
Wash with light this dark sickness from our eyes.

THOMAS R. SMITH

DAYS OF RAIN

Open me up to feel due words
—Phillip Booth, from Hope

I want the losing it all
as when it rains hard.
I want letting it all loose;
to open myself
to the only true opener
of my freer falling feeling.

I want that dense drape of
drenched space to drop
into the entire air,
the atmosphere, the ache, fall
there, drawn, down, drowned
into the lowest ground

of the great and good grieving,
soaked into that low place
of kind green grass
and further then,
into the darker grit that gathers it,
the one who finally gets it:

who becomes exactly what it is,
the one who lets grieving sound out
again, returns it, yet now, wholly held,
to this singular heart-of-mine

that might, may, must
grow greater through love's loss.

JOHN FOX

FAITH

I think continually of those who were truly great. . .
—Stephen Spender

I think continually of those who step forward
in spite of chasms to close for comfort
their feet keep vigil upon
the humble earth and all its tears,
the dark hungry tangled roots of
being alive, feet pushed down as if listening
to the presence of what finally matters:
fragile moments giving way like sand
kind voices green as grass
the deep strata of ageless strength
unseen. One step at a time,
even when their hearts, high up
in the spinning world are pounding or empty
of courage. Walking along the edge,
where something is felt underneath: the faith
the unknown alone can give, these,
the footprints I follow.

JOHN FOX

WHEN SOMEONE DEEPLY LISTENS TO YOU

When someone deeply listens to you
it is like holding out a dented cup
you've had since childhood
and watching it fill up with
cold, fresh water.
When it balances on top of the brim,
you are understood.
When it overflows and touches your skin,
you are loved.

When someone deeply listens to you
the room where you stay
starts a new life
and the place where you wrote
your first poem
begins to glow in your mind's eye.
It is as if gold has been discovered!

When someone deeply listens to you
your bare feet are on the earth
and a beloved land that seemed distant
is now at home within you.

JOHN FOX

LIFT UP THE BANNER

Lift up the banner of your heart boldly
and commit your very next step
to what you love most dearly.
Such a banner is for the greatness
of wildflowers kissing their way delicately
through glaciers, for the beauty
of the mountaintop from which your soul
undoubtedly has gazed.
The next step you take shall bring you home
if you but release your cares
and think instead that help has come,
as sure as the wind will fly the banner
that you have raised—
the quietness of a wind
in an unseen meadow that waves
the banner of who you are
with the whispered assurance that says:
I Am. Or the great, great wind
that fills ships sails announcing
your arrival to a throng of blue sky,
angelic presence's hushed in appreciation.
Your arrival to the new world of a new day,
the blessed shore rushing up to greet you.

JOHN FOX

WHEN JEWELS SING

Radiance results from earth's pressure,
life working on us with each moments precision
into clear cut uniqueness.

A community of precious human beings
with origins primitive and wild as diamonds.
Faceted by skilled and invisible hands that turn us
upon a wheel dusted with God's bright dark silence,
we become men and women joined to walk
swarthy, holy, original and transparent.

Catching first light of day upon ourselves,
our voices sing of truth and loveliness,
in response to vows first sung to us by stars.

JOHN FOX

A TRUTH THE HERON KNOWS

The woman, poised on the lip of a lake
grasps a truth the heron knows.

She is waiting for epiphany
standing in the gloaming,
skin white as feathers and fluttering.

Waiting for the emergence of light
through cloud. For the silver fin
which will break the lake's dark skin.

How motionless she is.
Only her mind moves.

The truth the heron knows
that to be still is to catch the dance.

Suspended creature, on the brink.
Body stock still, wings folded in.

Waiting to spear the sudden flourish
that breaks the lake's dark skin.

ARRIVAL

On arrival you will ascend into light
as if breaking water.
The ether will seem thinner
somehow, the sky more intact.

You will feel as if you are experiencing
the transition of a soul freed from flesh.

You will still have stones from the city
impaled in your shoes,
their weight a manacle
to your flight.

This is how it was for Eurydice,
before she plummeted back.

Her head birthing a brilliant expanse.
Her feet fettered by the dark.

ANNA SAUNDERS

THE RIVER SEEMS TO SAY

Leave your flotsam, float
like Ophelia, gazing up at the sky.

Leave behind on the bank
the prickly stick of 'I',
and glide.

Here, no reed beds
will catch you like a loose thread.

Bulrushes will act
only as exclamation marks
excited at your drift,

and the crows over-head
who manipulate eddies of air
will be envious

of the way the water works for you,
and how your limbs lie inert
in your effortless flight.

ANNA SAUNDERS

CRA COURT

From here it's difficult to tell
which tree houses his soul.

It's hard to tell them apart,
as they stand clustered,
darkness obscuring
any distinguishing marks.

But he is in there, boughs latticed
in the skies funeral-lace.

The tallest of them,
closest to the clouds
he is the one who makes the finest nest.

And as you come closer
you see the rooks argue
in his defence

before two hundred wings;
glossy and dark as Onyx

fan out and beat down,
and a Parliament
of black-clad creatures
make their exodus from court.

ANNA SAUNDERS

HE HAS GONE INTO A TREE

He's lithe and light, now he is dead,
and rises easily, losing the soil
from his soles.

Travelling up through roots
to bole and trunk,
he surges through heart wood
to break through the crown.

How easily he moves between worlds.
Scuttling up the axis
between earth and air.

He darts and spangles
like a jack lantern.

Who needs limbs?

He's reached the top
and nestles in.

Look—he's cupped
in the branches—an orb
which some may mistake
for the moon.

ANNA SAUNDERS

PORCH

after R.S. Thomas

How close do you feel to God?
asks the priest. As I sit with my back
to the altar, God answers for me,
throws open the locked door

of my heart, turns the heavy ring
of the handle, lifts the stiff catch,
takes away my breath on the swing
of smooth hinges, lets in the air

that is everywhere. God isn't arriving
nor leaving, through this four-chambered
porch under my ribs. He is the opening
and the door, the push and pulse

of whatever moves through me,
the whole red messiness of love.

LITANY FOR THE ANIMALS

For anteaters and ants, Abdulali's Wrinkled Frog and Abe's
                                        Salamander
Let us pray to the Lord

For all the birds of the air, buffalo that once filled the plains
for bees and their dances, for blue butterflies of our childhoods
Let us invoke the Goddess

For cattle incarcerated in mega-dairies, for cows with udders
scraping the ground,
for kind eyes of heifers and ebullience of bullocks
Let us beg for forgiveness

For dogs in their dogginess
wolves, coyotes, hyenas, hairless Mexican dogs, dogs on the streets
with the homeless, dogs by the hearth, at our heels with hearts full
of love
Let us give thanks and praise

For elephants with their graveyards and tears, tenderness and
listening feet
Let us be reverent and learn

For foxes, encroaching on cities, in dens in the woods,
for foxes, running in terror from the hounds
for foxes, fat-brushed and burnished in the field at dawn
Let us acknowledge complexity

For the forty endangered species of Galapagos Land Snail—
bulimulus adelphus, bulimulus darwinii, bulimulus nux, bulimulus
wolfi, et cetera
Let us wonder at Gaia

For wild horses, unshod, untamed, untethered, galloping over
the moor
Let us stand in admiration and awe

For horses with bit, bridle and saddle, whip, jump and stable
Let us hang our heads in shame

For the ibex, ibis, impala, iguana and iguanodon
Let us stop being an 'I' and turn into 'we'

For the jaguar alone in the empty forests of Guyana
Let us provide food and shelter

For the kangaroo, her pouch and her joey, her bounce and her
boing
For the koala beloved of children, for the kith and kin of the
animals
Let us smile unto the Lord

For the lionness and ladybird, the locust and limpet, for the lark and
his joyful song
*Let us sing … [sing] 'All you need is love .. All you need is love … All you
need is love, love. Love is all you need.*

For the Manx cat and maned wolf, mandrill and marsh deer
Let us revere the earth our mother, and all the mothers that gave us life

For the nuthatch in the garden
Let us see the miracle of small things

For the sight of an otter sliding slick as a shadow in the shallows
of the rich river
Let us sigh an Oh! of wonder

For parakeets, parrots, peacocks, pelicans, penguins and
peregrine falcons
Let us thank the Goddess for feathered beauty in all its forms

For rabbits, their reproductive vigour, their fluffy tails and soft
                                        noses
Let us learn gentleness

For the sixty five thousand animals in danger of extinction
Let us lament them, let us say; no, no, no, no …

For Tyrannosaurus Rex and all his brothers and sisters
Let us never forget

For unicorns and six-legged antelopes, Cheshire cats and
                                        dragons
Let us pay heed to our dreams

For the Variegated Spider Monkey, Venezuelan Wood-quail, Velvet
Worm and Visayan Warty Pig
Let us honour them by knowing their names

For the whales, the dolphins, all the cetaceans roaming our oceans,
for those in captivity
Let us always choose freedom

For the thud and sudden end of extinction, for the last creature
                                        of its kind
Mother Earth, help us make new life

For you, you, you and you,
Let us celebrate the web of creation [join hands]

For the zebra, zumbador, zebu and zho
*Let us know endings are beginnings in the circle of life
and remember ant-eaters and ants, Abdulali's Wrinkled Frog and
                                        Abe's Salamander.*

VICTORIA FIELD

AFTER THE WEDDING

Everywhere was Sunday-silent by the river in the early morning
as they slid towards me — twenty seven swans describing a heart,

each following the folded cup of the wings of the swan in front,
making a shape that's round, like valleys and hills, breasts and
                                                                roses,

smiles and eyes, then coming to an apex, like prayer and churches,
like an act of love, spears of irises bright and sharp in the water

each yellow beak leading, each long neck forward and yearning,
each pair of paddling feet, blessing the river, coming together

like a congregation witnessing love, honouring a rose-crowned
                                                                bride,
a groom, sheltering as an oak, complete and endless as a pair of
                                                                gold rings.

VICTORIA FIELD

FATHER

from a line by George Szirtes

My father carries me across a field.
How did you enter this field?
Foxily, through a hole in the hedge
Under cover of darkness and birds' nests.

My father carries me across a field.
What sort of field?
Tussocky, chaotic with cows,
Desire lines leading through brambles and gorse.

My father carries me across a field.
Are you too tired to walk?
I'm just a child who might go astray.
His strong arms hold me close to his heart.

My father carries me across a field.
Is he a farmer, your father?
No, he loves black earth, broad beans
Horses and beer, but the land isn't his.

My father carries me across a field.
And then?
He's opened a heavy gate and gone through
Disappeared down a deep lane among trees.

There's no one carrying me across a field.
Just a tweed cap, flat in my hands
Holding thoughts of winter days
And a faraway voice, calling the way.

VICTORIA FIELD

PETITION

In Cornwall, the saints are sleeping
under billowing dunes. Sand blew in
and blanketed the churches,
silenced the oratories and stilled the bell.

These are saints without armies,
drifting in on leaves or shells or stones,
their voices soft and strong and long as wind,
hearts smooth and white as bone.

There's no Augustinian turning from the world—
no need when world is a muddy path
with primroses, squat trees, deep creeks,
clefts in the cliffs and running surf.

Elsewhere, the saints are prodded
by police with bombs and guns.
Thirsty women walk miles to shrines,
mouths dried to silence by desert storms.

Here, bracken censes the holy wells
and pilgrims bring their private fears.
Torn rags hanging from the twigs
are damp with moss and prayers and tears.

Winds get ready to blow away the sand
and toll the bell for the limbless child.
The saints will rise and arm themselves
with gentleness, seek out the wells,

surprised to see, shimmering in dark water,
their half-forgotten face again
and there, among the heavy fronds,
miracles trickling with the rain.

VICTORIA FIELD

ARCHITECTURE OF LIGHT

When we come together and listen,
a voice wakes up inside.
Like Bach composing Cello
Suites—light made sound.

Blown away by this power,
head bowed, listening,
here I am—chrysalis to butterfly,
entering an architecture of light.

MAGGOT

Unfurling petals
expose me inert, naked,
soaked on my cushion.

I was here before
the flower chose red. I am
raw! The sun strikes sharp.

Burrow deep, wriggle
through the flower's sap to eat
and bathe at the heart.

KIM FRENCH

LUMBRICALS

for Jeanne

Small feather muscles in my hands
contract, expand, giving breath to
space. Palms spread, drawing from periphery
to diaphragm as my brain learns
new patterns, cutting below trauma.
If I let this wave of fear go through me
things change. I keep my space inside and out,
nervous system balanced not galvanised.
Resilient I own my inner world.

Resilient I own my inner world,
nervous system balanced not galvanised,
things change. I keep my space inside and out
if I let this wave of fear go through me.
New patterns, cutting below trauma
to diaphragm, as my brain learns
space. Palms spread, drawing from periphery,
contract, expand, giving breath to
small feather muscles in my hands.

KIM FRENCH

IN THE HOLDING SPACE

for John

In the darkness
that surrounds us
we are the sound
we are not the story
from one lifetime to the next.
The essence of ourselves
continuous from heaven to earth
from earth to heaven
on a path
with all those that have gone before –
artists, lovers, friends, children
we are not alone
leaping into the abyss.
Each night a little death
every day a journey
towards the spiral of life
beyond the everyday.
To communicate our intention
we are in the holding space.

We are in the holding space
to communicate our intention
beyond the everyday
towards the spiral of life.
Every day a journey,
each night a little death.
Leaping into the abyss
we are not alone –
artists, lovers, friends, children,

with all those that have gone before
on a path
from earth to heaven
continuous from heaven to earth.
The essence of ourselves
from one lifetime to the next —
we are not the story
we are the sound
that surrounds us
in the darkness.

KIM FRENCH

FULCRA

So firmly rooted in a body that does not exist,
transcend the solid experience of your body
as you have come to know it and move
its fulcra away from areas of past trauma
toward creating channels for incoming light.
Important now is to begin the dialogue,
the rest will follow with patience and caritas.

KIM FRENCH

THANK YOU!
(biographies below)

BIOGRAPHIES...

Sebastian Barker (d. 2014) was born in 1945 and educated in both the sciences and the arts, worked as a fireman, furniture restorer, freelance writer, editor and book expert in Sothebys. His poetry includes *Guarding the Border: Selected Poems* (Enitharmon, 1992), *The Dream of Intelligence* (1992), a long poem based on Nietzsche's life and works, *Damnatio Memoriae* (Enitharmon, 2004) and *The Land of Gold* (Enitharmon, 2014). He also wrote three collections of philosophical, theological and cultural essays. From 1988-1992 he was Chairman of the Poetry Society of Great Britain. A Hawthornden Fellow, he was elected a Fellow of the Royal Society of Literature in 1997 and in 2002 appointed successor of John Lehmann and Alan Ross as editor of The London Magazine, a post he held until 2008. In 1983, he bought and restored a ruin in the Greek mountains which became his second home.

Zanna Beswick (b. 1952) is a university lecturer and director in Drama and Theatre. For British television she has commissioned and/or produced over 200 hours of broadcast drama in series and serials ('the form best suited to television drama' she says). She has trained a stable of writers and editors for television. As a poet she considers the inner and outer worlds with a more contemplative energy. Her poetry has been published in *The Independent, Resurgence, Writing Women, Caduceus, The French Literary Review, Kindred Spirit, Chrysalis* and *Second Shift*, etc.; and in various anthologies. Her work has been shortlisted in the Arvon International Competition, Bath Poetry Competition, Mslexia, Expressions of Encephalitis, and Acumen, and has been broadcasted on Poetry Please (BBC Radio 4), and Poetry Marathon (Capital Radio London). She lives in NE Somerset.

Robert Bly (b. 1926) is the author of numerous books of poetry, including *The Light Around the Body*, winner of the National Book Award, and most recently *Stealing Sugar from the Castle: Selected and New Poems 1950-2013* and *Like the New Moon I Will Live My Life*. He is also the author of *Iron John: A Book About Men*, an international bestseller and a pioneering work in the men's movement. His awards include the Poetry Society of America's Frost Medal for distinguished lifetime achievement in poetry. He is the subject of a new documentary film, *A Thousand Years of Joy*. He lives in Minneapolis.

Janine Canan, poet and psychiatrist, volunteer for Amma'sEmbracing the World project, is the author of twenty booksincluding poetry, essays, stories, translations of Jammes and Lasker-Schueler, and award-winning anthologies, *She Rises like the Sun* and *Messages from Amma*. Canan's newest collections are *Mystic Bliss, Ardor: Poems of Life*, and *Garland of Love: 108 Sayings by Amma*. The poet lives in California's Valley of the Moon with her Samoyed companion, and can be visited at JanineCanan.com or on Facebook.

Jeni Couzyn (b. 1942) began her working life as a free-lance poet in London, doing readings, broadcasts, and teaching. She published collections with Cape, Heinemann, The Women's Press and Bloodaxe, and in Canada with Anansi and JJ Douglas. Her book *In the Skin House* has a foreword by the Sufi mystic Llewellyn Vaughan Lee. In 1999, she set up the First People Centre in the remote Karoo village of Nieu Bethesda—a project to assist /Xam Bushman survivors of historical genocide in her native country, South Africa. www.nieubethesda.org The Centre and its people have been central to her work for the last seventeen years, along with her work as a psychotherapist. Her poems are often published in the magazine "*Sufi*" and are forthcoming in *Temenos* and *Resurgence* magazines.

Jenny D'Angelo (b. 1946) poet, editor, healer, Angel Scribe. She was adopted as granddaughter/next of kin by Dorie D'Angelo, "the Angel Lady of Carmel," in 1983. Before meeting Dorie, she was International Editor for Maharishi Mahesh Yogi, who brought Transcendental Meditation to the world. Her poems have appeared in numerous international collections. Her most recent book is *Connect with Your Angels: A Guide for Everyone* (Robertson, 2014). Jenny has presented in the U.S., Switzerland, Denmark, Italy, the Netherlands, and Sweden. She lives on California's central coast. She blogs at: angelsinlight.wordpress.com

Hilary Davies (b. 1954) has three collections of poetry from Enitharmon: *The Shanghai Owner of the Bonsai Shop, In a Valley of This Restless Mind*, and *Imperium*. A fourth collection, *Exile and the Kingdom*, is due out from Enitharmon this September. Hilary won an Eric Gregory award in 1983, has been a Hawthornden Fellow, Chairman of the Poetry Society, and 1st prizewinner in the Cheltenham Literature Festival poetry competition. She was Head of Languages at St. Paul's Girls' School, London, for 19 years and is currently Royal Literary Fund Fellow at King's College, London. Hilary was married to the poet and editor, Sebastian Barker (The London Magazine), who died in January 2014. http://www.enitharmon.co.uk/pages/authors/author_details.asp?AuthorID=17

Aidan Andrew Dun (b. 1952), was born in London, spent a fantastical childhood in the West Indies and knew his calling for poetry from an early age. Returning to the UK as a teenager in '68 to live with his inspirational grandmother, dancer Marie Rambert, he briefly attended Highate School but left without A-levels after taking (perhaps too seriously) the role of the rebel-chieftan Aufidius in Coriolanus. After several years travelling the world with a guitar AAD was drawn back to London to explore the psychogeography of Kings Cross, magnet to other visionaries before him. Surviving - and working - in squat-culture for 15 years, he slowly gestated *Vale Royal*, an epic poem which dreams of transforming an urban wasteland into a transcultural zone of canals at the heart of London. In 1995 Allen Ginsberg flew in from NY to perform - with Paul McCartney - at the launch of *Vale Royal* at the Royal Albert Hall in a reprise of the Wholly Communion event of 30 years earlier. Launching his second epic poem *India Cantos* (Universal) in 2002 AAD accomplished an American tour, reading in New York, Santa Fe and San Francisco (at City Lights Bookshop). AAD has read alongside David Gascoigne, Ben Okri, Iain Sinclair and Andrew Motion. In 2008 he lectured at the British Library on The Kings Cross Mysteries. Numerous short (and some longer) poems have appeared in *The London Magazine, English, The Cortland Review, The Salzburg Review, Tears in the Fence, Resurgence, Scintilla* et al. In 2005 AAD undertook a special commission for The Wordsworth Trust. *The Uninhabitable City* (Goldmark) was published in 2005; *Salvia Divinorum* (Goldmark) appeared in 2007. *McCool, a verse-novel in 264 sonnets*, followed from the same publisher in 2010. Appearing in 2016 (from Skyscraper in the UK and Interlink in the USA) is *Unholyland* a verse-novel in 800 sonnets set in Palestine/Israel. Heathcote Williams describes *Unholyland* as 'a pyrotechnic, apocalyptic dance.... a powerful meditation on the place where civilization began and where it could end.'

Diana Durham (b. 1954) is the author of three poetry collections: *Sea of Glass* (Diamond Press), *To the End of the Night* (Northwoods Press) & *Between Two Worlds— sonnets* (Chrysalis Poetry): the nonfiction *The Return of King Arthur* (Tarcher/Penguin) and a debut novel *The Curve of the Land* (Skylight Press). Her poetry has featured in numerous journals and anthologies in the UK and USA. Diana was a member of the London poetry performance group Angels of Fire (with Jay Ramsay); in New Hampshire she founded 3 Voices, with two other women writers. She holds a BA in English Lit from University College London, and was a Visiting Research Associate at the Womens' Studies Research Center, Brandeis University. Diana is also trained in the healing practice of Attunement. Diana is British, but she and her family live in Portsmouth, New Hampshire. www.dianadurham.net

Victoria Field (b. 1963) is a writer and poetry therapist. Her most recent collection of poetry *The Lost Boys*, Waterloo Press, 2013 won the Holyer an Gof Award for Poetry and Drama. She has had poetry and short fiction commissioned by BBC Radio 3 and 4 and is also a playwright and former writer-in-residence at Truro Cathedral. Her memoir of pilgrimage and marriage *Baggage: A Book of Leavings* was published in 2016 by Francis Boutle. She's a mentor-supervisor for the International Federation for Biblio-Poetry Therapy www.thepoetrypractice.co.uk

Rose Flint (b. 1944) is a writer and art therapist. She has taught Creative Writing for Therapeutic Purposes and works in hospitals, healthcare and the community. An international prize-winning poet, her work has been widely published in anthologies and magazines including *Poetry Review* (London) and *Scintilla* (Wales). She has published six collections: *Blue Horse of Morning, Firesigns, Nekyia, Mother of Pearl, A Prism for the Sun,* and *Grace, Breath, Bone, poems for the Goddess.* As a committed Green Party voter, her writing is centred on earth-based spirituality. She lives in Somerset.

John Fox (b. 1955) is a poet and certified poetry therapist. John is author of *Poetic Medicine: The Healing Art of Poem-making* and *Finding What You Didn't Lose: Expressing Your Truth and Creativity Through Poem-Making.* His work is featured in the PBS documentary Healing Words: Poetry and Medicine. His essays have appeared in numerous books on subjects of education, mindfulness, expressive therapy, creativity, medicine, healing & spirituality, etc. A chapbook of John's poems, *The Only Gift to Bring,* was published by Seasonings Press in 2015. John is currently adjunct associate professor at the California Institute of Integral Studies in San Francisco, CA where he has taught since 2000. John is Founder and President of The Institute for Poetic Medicine which funds poetry projects for marginalized people. Find out more about his work at www.poeticmedicine.org

Kim French (b. 1976) is a writer and movement-practitioner living in London. She has previously lived in Ireland for ten years and has travelled extensively around the world. Driven by a belief in the body's intrinsic desire for wholeness and its ability to facilitate its own healing, her writing is currently influenced by her studies in Continuum, Body-Mind-Centering and movement-improvisation.

She is currently in a writing class with Jo Shapcott at Faber, and is at work on her first poetry collection *The Architecture of Light*.

David Gascoyne (1916-2001) had his first book *Roman Balcony* published when he was only 16 (in 1932). He was the youngest of the writers in Paris at the time of Anais Nin and Henry Miller, and wrote some remarkable surrealist poetry. After the War he developed his own particular gravitas as a poet in a religious and spiritual context before a breakdown left him hospitalized for some years. He latterly lived with his wife Judy on the Isle of Wight, where he continued to translate Modern French poetry. He was also a close friend of Kathleen Raine. His *Collected Poems* (OUP, 1965) is the source for the poems in this anthology.

Ivan M. Granger (b. 1969) is a poet and modern mystic. He is the founder and editor of the Poetry Chaikhana (www.poetry-chaikhana.com), an online resource for the exploration of sacred poetry from the world's great spiritual traditions. His poetry and translations have been published in *Real Thirst: Poetry of the Spiritual Journey* (Poetry Chaikhana), *For Lovers of God Everywhere: Poems of Christian Mystics* (Hay House, ed. Roger Housden), and *Poems of Awakening* (Outskirts Press, ed. Betsy Small). He is the editor of *The Longing in Between: Sacred Poetry from Around the World* (Poetry Chaikhana). Mr. Granger lives in Colorado.

Andrew Harvey (co-editor: b. 1952) is an internationally acclaimed poet, novelist, translator, mystical scholar, and spiritual teacher. He has published over 20 books including his book on *Rumi The Way of Passion* (1994), his book on *Jesus Son of Man* (1998), *Sun at Midnight* (2002), *The Hope—a Guide to Sacred Activism* (Hay House, 2009), and his newest book *Radical Passion: Sacred Love and Wisdom in Action* (North Atlantic Books, 2012) which is also an anthology of his prose. Harvey was a Fellow of All Souls College Oxford from 1972-1986 and has taught at Oxford University, Cornell University, The California Institute of Integral Studies, and the University of Creation Spirituality, as well as, various spiritual centers throughout the United

States. He was the subject of the 1993 BBC film documentary The Making of a Modern Mystic. He is the Founder of the Institute for Sacred Activism. His website is www.andrewharvey.net.

Alan Jackson (b. 1938). A Scot. Lives in Edinburgh. AJ writes: In 1968 after a reading in Aberdeen a man in the audience asked me: 'Why do you write poetry, Mr Jackson?' Inwardly I thought 'Bloody hell! What a question!' but straightaway I answered: When I was about fifteen the gods looked down on me and one said What can we do for this poor wretch? After a pause another replied: Let's give him poetry and see what he makes of it. www.alanjacksonpoet.com

Georgi Y. Johnson (b. 1967), writer and spiritual teacher, was born in Sheffield in 1967. Now based in the Middle East, she gives seminars worldwide on awakening and spiritual healing together with her partner Bart ten Berge. She is author of: *I AM HERE - Opening the Windows of Life & Beauty*, a book inquiring into the trilogy of consciousness, awareness and emptiness as forms of perception. www.iamherelife.com

Peter Owen Jones (b. 1957) grew up in the English countryside. He started writing poetry in his late teens when he was living chaotically in London. His deep love for the natural world is expressed in his latest book *Pathlands* (Rider, 2015). He is also the author of *Letters from an Extreme Pilgrim* (which records his time spent in the Sinai Desert), and *Psalm*. He has presented several documentaries for the BBC including Extreme Pilgrim, How to Live a Simple Life, and Around the World in 80 Faiths and is currently, as Vicar of Firle, the parish priest for three rural parishes on the Sussex Downs.

Irina Kuzminsky (b. 1959) has spent her life in a quest for the feminine dimension of God, and poetry, dance and music are an intrinsic part of that journey. Born in Australia of White Russian descent, she combines classical music and dance training with an academic background, including a scholarship to Oxford where she wrote her doctorate on the 'Language of Women' and was elected Junior Research Fellow in Humanities at Wolfson College. Poetry publications include *Dancing with Dark Goddesses, light muses* (with artist Jan Delaney), *Into the Silence, poems and articles in Soul of the Earth, Esoteric Quarterly, Acumen, Caduceus, Poetrix,* and others. As Irinushka she has released three CDs of her poetry set to music, *Would That I Could, Roads Travelled* which featured on the ZoneMusicReporter top 100 chart for New Age music, and *Orpheus Sings.* Her one woman dance, poetry and music fusion show *Dancing with Dark Goddesses* has been seen in New York, Melbourne, Germany and the UK. www.vimeo.com/86810433, www.irinakuzminsky.com; www.soundcloud.com/irinushka

Paul Matthews (b. 1944) lives in Forest Row, Sussex, UK with his Californian wife. His inspirational books on the creative process, *Sing Me the Creation,* and *Words in Place* (both available from Hawthorn Press) arose out of many years work as lecturer and resident poet at Emerson College, Forest Row, Sussex. His poetry, gathered in *The Ground that Love Seeks,* and *Slippery Characters* (Five Seasons Press), is strongly influenced by American poets, Robert Duncan in particular. www.paulmatthewspoetry.co.uk

Niall McDevitt (b. 1967) is an Irish poet living in London, author of two collections, *b/w* (Waterloo Press, 2010) and *Porterloo* (International Times, 2012). He is an urban explorer who follows the trails of Shakespeare, Blake, Rimbaud, Yeats and many others, in London and beyond. His essays on David Gascoyne have been published in *The Fiend, The Wolf,* and elsewhere. He hosted An Evening Without David Gascoyne at Pentameters Theatre in 2012 which also included Jeremy Reed, Hilary Davies and Robert Fraser. His third book is about Jerusalem and is forthcoming from Robert Montgomery's New River Press.

Jehanne Mehta (b. 1941) is a singer-songwriter and poet, focussing especially on our connection with Nature and the Earth. She has also developed a unique form of sound healing, using her voice.

She has led workshops on the sound work and has also inspired creative writing in a group context. With her group 'Earthwards' she has recorded several CDs and has five published collections of poems: *The Burning Word, Nest Edge, The Difficult Gate, Walking Two Ways, Heart of Yew*. She has had poems published in various journals including *Tears* in the Fence and has contributed articles and poems regularly to the *Cygnus Review*. www.jehannemehta.com

Gabriel Bradford Millar (b. 1944) is a renegade American. She graduated cum laude from Barnard College, Columbia University and did post-grad work at Edinburgh, where she read with Norman MacCaig and The Heretics, and was interviewed on BBC Radio Scotland. She's published six books including *The Saving Flame* (Five Seasons Press, 2000) and her *Selected Poems Crackle of Almonds* (Awen, 2012) and given scores of readings, sharing the stage several times with Kathleen Raine. With Jay Ramsay she co-founded Celebration of the Word in Stroud, Gloucestershire: a fertile alternative community where she's lived for many years. She has two grown-up daughters and two stepsons.

Helen Moore (b. 1971) is an award-winning ecopoet and socially engaged artist based in Somerset, UK. Her debut poetry collection, *Hedge Fund, And Other Living Margins* (Shearsman Books, 2012), was described by Alasdair Paterson as being "in the great tradition of visionary politics in British poetry." Her second collection, *ECOZOA* (Permanent Publications, 2015), which responds to Thomas Berry's vision of the 'Ecozoic Era', has been acclaimed by John Kinsella, as "a milestone in the journey of ecopoetics". Helen also makes video poetry with Howard Vause; their film 'Greenspin' was awarded 3rd prize in the Liberated Words International Poetry Film Festival in 2013: http://vimeo.com/69228739 Helen's website is: www.natures-words.co.uk

Lisa Page (b.1972) is an international speaker, author, poet, and Sacred Intimacy Mentor who has been passionately exploring the deeper truths of life, love and intimacy for more than twenty years.

For over fifteen years she's worked with women and couples from around the world as the Founder of SoulSatisfactionForWomen.com and Co-Founder of LivingLovingDeeper.com weaving a unique blend of relational psychology and somatic-spiritual principles and practices. Lisa is the author of training programmes such as *Breathe Baby Breathe, Life, Love & Intimacy, Intimate Conversations with Great Mystics, Wise Teachers & Everyday Lovers*, the co-author of *Picture Them Naked* and the producer of the film series in production, Intimate Conversations with Great Mystics, Wise Teachers & Everyday Lovers which can be found at LisaPage.com.au. Lisa is also the Creatrix of EmbodySHE®, a unique body of transformational women's work grounded in feminine embodiment practice, powerful breath-work, original-wild-free-movement, artistic offering and sacred ritual. Lisa lives on the beach in South Australia with her partner and teenage son, but as a self confessed WanderLuster still finds any excuse to travel the world for work, pleasure and exploration.

Sally Purcell (1944-1998) was an Oxford-based poet and translator, after attending the University where she studied Medieval French. Her collections included *The Holly Queen* (1971), *Dark of Day* (1977), *Lake and Labyrinth* (1985) and *Fossil Unicorn* (1997) before her *Collected Poems* (2001), edited by Peter Jay at Anvil with a Foreword by Marina Warner. Geoffrey Godbert also published a pamphlet of her work at Greville Press in the 1980s, admiring how it stood apart from 20th century realism in emphasizing the imagination and inner life. She also translated *Amorgos* (1944), the long surreal poem by the Greek poet Nikos *Gatsos* (Anvil Press Poetry, 2000) to stunning effect.

Kathleen Raine (1907-2003) was a Blake scholar, a Yeats scholar, and founder of the journal Temenos and the Temenos Academy. Gavin Maxwell's bestselling Ring of Bright Water about his beloved pet otter took its title from one of her poems at the time. Kathleen wrote three remarkable volumes of autobiography where she fuses science and mysticism; she is unique in that. Her first collection *Stone and Flower* (1943) was followed by *Living in Time* (1946), *The*

Pythoness (1949), *The Year One* (1952), *The Hollow Hill* (1965), *The Lost Country* (1971), *On a Deserted Shore* (1973), *The Oval Portrait* (1977), *The Oracle in the Heart* (1980), *The Presence* (1987), and *Living with Mystery* (1992). Her Collected Poems are published in the US by Counterpoint, Washington. She was awarded the Queen's Gold Medal in 2003.

Jay Ramsay (co-editor: b. 1958) is the author of 35 books of poetry, non-fiction, and classic Chinese translation including *The White Poem, Alchemy; Crucible of Love–the alchemy of passionate relationships, Tao Te Ching, I Ching—the shamanic oracle of change, The Poet in You* (his correspondence course, since 1990), *Kingdom of the Edge—Selected Poems 1980-1998, Out of Time—1998-2008, Anamnesis—the remembering of soul* (in residence at St. James', Piccadilly, London) and *Places of Truth* (2009). His latest collections are *Agistri Notebook* (KFS, 2014), *Monuments* (Waterloo Press, 2014), *Surgery* (Yew Tree Press, 2015), and also the *The Most Venerable Book, Shang Shu*—with Martin Palmer (Penguin Classics). He is also poetry editor of Caduceus magazine, and works in private practice as a UKCP accredited psychosynthesis psychotherapist and healer, running poetry and personal development workshops worldwide. www.jayramsay.co.uk

Alan Rycroft (b. 1957) was born in London, and though based in Bristol with his family, life has often taken him on a planetary odyssey. Being a qualified teacher, he has an MA in Applied Linguistics, and he has long been engaged in teaching English and English Literature in universities in the Middle and Far East. He has been much privileged and enriched to imbibe and interact with so many cultural influences and faith traditions globally. 'And all the while, poetry (he says) has quietly distilled it all, a constant companion and mentor, a profound and rich internalized form of therapy and illumination, as well as craft. And simultaneously it's been questioning and quest; a form of channelling and conversing with Spirit, the multidimensional voices of the voice, by turns human and every day, mythic, shamanistic, philosophical and spiritually enlightening'. His collection *At the Steep Face of Your Heart* is forthcoming (arycroft@yahoo.com).

Chris Saade (b. 1950) is a former therapist and trained therapists and coaches in the method of "Individual Authenticity and Global Solidarity." Saade offers personal psychological and spiritual coaching, and cutting edge workshops. He has led more than 200 retreats. For over a decade during the Lebanese war, Chris Saade was involved in peace and humanitarian work. The challenges of those difficult years taught him to approach tragedy through heart and service, leading him to develop a great respect for freedom, authenticity, diversity, and a passion for justice, especially for children. Saade has directed three non-profits. In addition to being the co-director of The Olive Branch Center with his wife, Jessie Thompson (www.theolivebranchcenter.net), Saade is the author of *Second Wave Spirituality: Passion for Peace, Passion for Justice*; and *Prayers of Peace and Justice*; and also *Prayers from the Heart*. Together with Andrew Harvey he has co-created two CD sets: An Evolutionary Vision of Relationships as well as Sacred Activism and the Epic Spirituality of Love. Saade currently has five manuscripts either under contract or in progress. Many of them are in collaboration with visual artists. Saade resides in San Diego.

Anna Saunders (b. 1965) is the author of *Communion*, (Wild Conversations Press), *Struck*, (Pindrop Press), *Kissing the She Bear*, (Wild Conversations Press), *Burne Jones and the Fox*, (Indigo Dreams), and *Kissing the She Bear* (Wild Conversations Press, 2015). She has had poems published in journals and anthologies which include *Ambit, The North, Amaryllis, Iota, New Walk Magazine, Caduceus, Envoi, The Wenlock Anthology 2014* and *The Museum of Light*. Anna holds a Masters in Creative and Critical Writing from The University of Gloucestershire. She is also the founder and CEO of Cheltenham Poetry Festival.

Henry Shukman (b. 1962) is the resident Zen teacher at Mountain Cloud Zen Center in Santa Fe, New Mexico, where he lives, and is an associate master of Sanbo Zen of Kamakura, Japan, studying under Yamada Ryo'un Roshi. He's also a writer and poet; his poetry collection *In Dr No's Garden* (Jonathan Cape) was Book of the Year in the London Guardian and Times, and his novel *Sandstorm* (also Cape) won the Author's Club First Novel Award, and his third novel *The Lost City* (Knopf) was a New York Times Editor's Choice. He is married to the artist Clare Dunne, with two sons. www.mountaincloud.org

Thomas R. Smith (b. 1948) is a poet, essayist, editor, and teacher living in western Wisconsin. His books of poetry include *The Foot of the Rainbow* and *The Glory* (both from Red Dragonfly Press), and he has edited, among other books, *Airmail: The Letters of Robert Bly and Tomas Tranströmer* (Graywolf in the US and Bloodaxe in the UK). He is an environmental activist and holds with the French poet Francis Ponge that the artist "must take the world into the shop for repairs, piece by piece as he or she finds it." www.thomasrsmithpoet.com

William Stafford (1914-1993) received the Robert Frost Medal in 1993 having published over sixty-five collections of poetry and prose. His first major collection *Traveling Through the Dark* won the National Book Award in 1963. A close friend of Robert Bly, Stafford was born in Kansas and spent most of his life in Oregon. Describing himself as one of "the quiet of the land", Stafford was a conscientious objector during World War II and a pacifist, while his work is rooted in the landscapes of the American West. He was appointed Consultant in Poetry to the Library of Congress (a position now know as Poet Laureate) in 1970, and named Poet Laureate of Oregon in 1975. Other awards included a Guggenheim Fellowship, a Shelley Memorial Award and a Western States Lifetime Achievement Award in Poetry.

Mirabai Starr (b. 1961) is a critically acclaimed author and translator of sacred literature. She teaches and speaks widely on contemplative practice, interspiritual experience, and the transformational power of loss. Her works include translations of *Dark Night of the Soul* by

John of the Cross, *The Interior Castle* and *The Book of My Life*, by Teresa of Avila and *The Showings of Julian of Norwich*, poetry collection *Mother of God Similar to Fire* (in collaboration with iconographer, William Hart McNichols), *Contemplations* and *Living Wisdom* (Sounds True), *God of Love: A Guide to the Heart of Judaism, Christianity and Islam*, and *Caravan of No Despair: A Memoir of Loss and Transformation*.

Thanissara (b. 1956), poet, Dharma teacher, author, and activist, is originally from London. She trained in the Thai Forest Tradition of Ajahn Chah for 12 years as a Buddhist nun and teaches meditation internationally. She is co-founder, with her partner and husband Kittisaro, of Dharmagiri Insight Meditation Centre on the border of Lesotho and South Africa, and Chattanooga Insight, Tennessee. Her work in South Africa, since 1994, involves teaching meditation, Buddhism, and therapeutic and mindfulness approaches to healing. She continues to fund-raise and support community uplift projects, particularly in response to the AIDS pandemic, in rural KwaZulu Natal. She is also core teacher at Insight Meditation Society, Massachusetts, and affiliated teacher at Spirit Rock and Insight Yoga Institute, California. Thanissara has an MA in Mindfulness Psychotherapy Practice from the Karuna Institute, South Devon, UK, and is author of poetry books *Garden of the Midnight Rosary* and *The Heart of the Bitter Almond Hedge Sutra*. She co-authored *Listening to the Heart, A Contemplative Journey to Engaged Buddhism* with Kittisaro. Her latest book is *Time to Stand Up, An Engaged Buddhist Manifesto for Our Earth, The Buddha's Life* and *Message Through Feminine Eyes* (2015).

Lewis Thompson (1909-1949) died in Benares, India in 1949, aged only 40. Almost unknown in his lifetime, he is a remarkable mystical 'pilgrim poet' whose work has been gathered and edited posthumously by Richard Lannoy and also championed by Andrew Harvey. *Black Sun*, his Collected Poems (which includes his long poem 'Black Angel'), is published by Hohm Press, Prescott, Arizona (2001). Thompson was a meticulous craftsman who also wrote voluminous journals as well as his prose work Mirror to the Light in which he reflects on the spiritual life and writing.

Jennifer Doane Upton (b. 1947) was born in eastern Kentucky and studied under Wendell Berry at the University of Kentucky. In 1972 she moved to California where she studied poetry with Jack Gilbert; she returned to Kentucky in 2004. Her books are: *Dark Way to Paradise: Dante's Inferno in Light of the Spiritual Path* (Sophia Perennis, 2005); *Black Sun: Poems 1965-1985*, (Finishing Line Press, 2014, by whose permission these poems are reprinted); and *The Ordeal of Mercy: Dante's Purgatorio in Light of the Spiritual Path* (Angelico Press, 2015). Her books on the Divine Comedy are dedicated to recovering a lost tradition: Christianity.

Charles Upton (b. 1948) is a poet, activist, protégé of Beat Generation poet Lew Welch, veteran of the psychedelic counterculture of the 60's, and a lifelong student of traditional metaphysics and comparative religion. He's published 4 books of poetry and 13 on metaphysics, mythopoetic exegesis, spiritual psychology and 'metaphysics and social criticism'. His short epic *Panic Grass* was published by City Lights Books in 1968. In 1988 he entered Islam, joined the Sufis, and discovered the metaphysics of the 'Traditionalist School'—René Guénon, Ananda Coomaraswamy, Frithjof Schuon. His first Traditionalist book was *The System of Antichrist: Truth and Falsehood in Postmodernism and the New Age* (2001). He moved to Lexington, Kentucky with his wife Jennifer in 2004. In 2013 be co-founded the Covenants Initiative, an international movement of Muslims to defend persecuted Christians. www.charles-upton.com

Dorothy Walters Ph.D. (b. 1928) lives and writes in Colorado. A long time lover of nature, of mystical poetry, and mysticism itself, she strives to contribute to the light now spreading in the midst of a dark time. Many years ago she experienced spontaneous Kundalini awakening, an event that totally changed her life. Her poetry grows from this continuing experience, and she is often visited by the

Beloved. She strongly believes in following the direction of the "guru" within, rather than the directives of a particular teacher or teaching. She also believes that the globe is currently undergoing spiritual awakening leading to universal evolution of consciousness. Dorothy has published five books of mystical poetry plus a spiritual autobiography, including *Marrow of Flame, Poems of the Spiritual Journey* (second edition); *A Cloth of Fine Gold, Poems of the Inner Journey; The Ley Lines of the Soul, Poems of Ecstasy and Ascension; Penelope's Loom, Poems of Turning Matter into Spirit; Some Kiss We Want, Poems Selected and New*. Her account of her Kundalini awakening is entitled *Unmasking the Rose, A Record of a Kundalini Initiation*. Dorothy Walters, PhD. www.kundalinisplendor.blogspot.com

Philip Wells (b. 1962) performs as The Fire Poet everywhere from Buckingham Palace to Canterbury Cathedral. Pioneer of interactive poetry with special needs children, he is poet-in-residence at Chelsea Hospital School and St Ann's School, London. His latest poetry collection is *The Night Without Dawn* (Albion, 2013). He walked 1000 miles barefoot on a bardic pilgrimage around Britain in 2014 and plans to walk barefoot from London to Rome in 2018.

PERMISSIONS & ACKNOWLEDGEMENTS

Special thanks to Kermit E. Heartsong at Tayen Lane, and Nora Boxer for her editing expertise, refining and polishing this as close to a gem as she could possibly make it. Also to Irina Kuzminsky for her help in getting it into final and coherent form. And to all the poets for their enthusiasm, willingness, support and generosity.

Every effort has been made to acknowledge copyrighted material. Any omissions will of course be rectified in future editions.

Sebastian Barker's poems appear with the kind permission of Hilary Davies, his widow, and also Enitharmon Press. They are taken from *Guarding the Border—Selected Poems* (1992), *The Hand in the Well* (1996), *Damnatio Memoriae* (2004), and *The Land of Gold* (2014).

Zanna Beswick's poems are taken from *Earth Ascending* (Stride), *3x4* (Raunchland), *The Listening Walk* (Bath Poetry Cafe) and *The Book of Love and Loss* (Belgrave Press).

Robert Bly's poems are taken from *Loving a Woman in Two Worlds* (HarperCollins, 1985), and *The Insanity of Empire* (Ally Press, 2004) reprinted with his kind permission. Thanks also to Thomas R. Smith for his assistance here.

Jeni Couzyn's poems, first published by Bloodaxe (1985, 1993), appear with her kind permission. For further permissions, please contact Tina Betts at Andrew Mann (tina@andrewmann.co.uk).

Jenny D'Angelo's poems "Saved" and "The Fragile Openness" were previously published in *Connect with Your Angels: A Guide for Everyone* (Robertson Publishing, 2014).

Hilary Davies' poems appear with the kind permission of Enitharmon Press.

Victoria Field's poems appear with the kind permission of Simon Jenner at Waterloo Press (Hove) and fal publications (Canterbury). www.waterloopresshove.co.uk

Rose Flint's *Firesigns* was first published by the University of Salzburg, 'Elements of Healing' is taken from *A Prism for the Sun* (Oversteps), 'Spirit Paths' from *Mother of Pearl* (PS Avalon), and 'Walking with Spiderwoman' and 'May Tide' from *Grace, Breath, Bone* (Wildish Press).

David Gascoyne's poems appear with the kind permission of Stephen Stuart-Smith and Enitharmon Press, London.

Irina Kuzminsky's poem 'She rides' first appeared in *Dancing with Dark Goddesses* (Awen, 2009), 'Epiphany' *is from "light muses blog"* (with artist Jan Delaney, Naditu Press, 2011), while 'The pure are...' was first published in the Fall 2012 issue of the *Esoteric Quarterly*.

Paul Matthews' poems 'The Living Room', 'In the Grass this Morning', 'The Kingdom that I Left Behind' appeared in *The Ground that Love Seeks* (Five Seasons Press). 'Rain at Midnight' appeared in *Slippery Characters* (Five Seasons Press).

Niall McDevitt: thanks to *London Magazine, International Times, Waterloo Press*, and *Scintilla* for publishing some of these poems.

"Ivan M. Granger's poem "Bent" and translation of "The fire rises in me" are published in Real Thirst: Poetry of the Spiritual Journey (Poetry Chaikhana, 2012). All other poems and translations are featured on the Poetry Chaikhana website (www.poetry-chaikhana.com)."

Jehanne Mehta's poems 'Seek not to hold her', 'Tympanum' and 'Soil' are all from *The Burning Word*, published by The Diamond Press, 1991. '*Sonnet*' is from *A Way to Meet* 1999.

Helen Moore's poems are taken from her second collection *ECOZOA* (Permanent Publications, 2015).

Sally Purcell's poems appear with the kind permission of Peter Jay at Anvil Press, London.

Kathleen Raine's poems appear with the kind permission of Brian Keeble for the Literary Estate of Kathleen Raine and Golgonooza Press, Ipswich; and are copyright 2000.

Jay Ramsay's poems are taken from *Kingdom of the Edge* (Element Books, 1999) and *Monuments* (Waterloo Press, 2014). They have also appeared in International Times (www.internationaltimes.it).

Anna Saunders' 'Arrival', 'A Truth the Heron Knows' and 'The River Seems to Say' are all taken from *Communion* (Wild Conversations Press, 2011). 'He Has Gone into a Tree' and 'Cra Court' are from Wild Conversations Press (April 2015).

Thomas R. Smith's 'At the Lincoln Memorial' and 'Julia Butterfly Hill' are reprinted from *The Glory* (Red Dragonfly Press, 2015).

Mirabai Starr's poems are taken from *Mother of God Similar to Fire* (in collaboration with iconographer, William Hart McNichols) (Orbis Books, 2010) www.amazon.com/Mother-Similar-Fire-William- Lewis Thompson's poems appear with the kind permission of Regina at Hohm Press (Prestcott, Arizona— www.hohmpress.com).

Jennifer Doane Upton's poems are taken from *Black Sun* which is re-published by Finishing Line Press (kevinmmaines@aol.com).

Thanissara's poem is taken from *The Heart of the Bitter Almond Hedge Sutra* Sacred Mountain Press, 2013 & CreateSpace

Independent Publishing Platform. Quote inspired by //Kabbo of the First Sitting There People (/Xam of Southern Africa), thanks to Alan James and University of KwaZulu Natal Press.

Henry Shukman's "Wind in Trees" was published in the Times Literary Supplement, London

Charles Upton's 3 poems are from *The Wars of Love and Other Poems* (Sophia Perennis, 2011), and 'Our real fear....' and 'The greatest beauty....' are from the short epic "The Wars of Love" specifically.

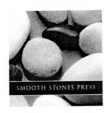

SMOOTH STONES PRESS

DIAMOND
CUTTERS

EDITED
& INTRODUCED BY

ANDREW HARVEY
& JAY RAMSAY

CPSIA information can be obtained at www.ICGtesting.com
Printed in the USA
LVOW08*2345170816

500811LV00002B/3/P